# Health IT as a Tool
# for Prevention in
# Public Health Policies

# Health IT as a Tool for Prevention in Public Health Policies

Divya Srinivasan Sridhar

CRC Press
Taylor & Francis Group
Boca Raton London New York

CRC Press is an imprint of the
Taylor & Francis Group, an **informa** business

A PRODUCTIVITY PRESS BOOK

CRC Press
Taylor & Francis Group
6000 Broken Sound Parkway NW, Suite 300
Boca Raton, FL 33487-2742

© 2014 by Taylor & Francis Group, LLC
CRC Press is an imprint of Taylor & Francis Group, an Informa business

No claim to original U.S. Government works

Printed on acid-free paper

International Standard Book Number-13: 978-1-4822-1474-1 (Paperback)

---

**Library of Congress Cataloging-in-Publication Data**

---

Sridhar, Divya Srinivasan, author.
  Health IT as a tool for prevention in public health policies / Divya Srinivasan Sridha.
  p. ; cm.
  Health information technology as a tool for prevention in public health policies
  Includes bibliographical references and index.
  ISBN 978-1-4822-1474-1 (alk. paper)
  I. Title. II. Title: Health information technology as a tool for prevention in public health policies.
  [DNLM: 1.  United States. Health Information Technology for Economic and Clinical Health Act. 2.  United States. Patient Protection and Affordable Care Act. 3.  Health Impact Assessment--United States. 4.  Medical Informatics--trends--United States. 5. Health Policy--United States. 6.  Healthcare Disparities--United States.  W 84.4 AA1]

  R858.A1
  610.285--dc23                                                                    2013032649

---

**Visit the Taylor & Francis Web site at**
**http://www.taylorandfrancis.com**

**and the CRC Press Web site at**
**http://www.crcpress.com**

This book is dedicated to the two most important men in my life—my brother, Aditya Srinivasan, and my husband, Badri Sridhar. They have provided me with the gifts of love and laughter, more so than any others in my life. I could see the light at the end of the tunnel when writing this book because of them.

# Contents

# Preface

## The PPACA and a New Focus on Prevention

The passing in 2010 of the Patient Protection and Affordable Care Act (PPACA) has produced a significant set of objectives for the United States and, indirectly, for the entire world. The PPACA works to produce solutions to a number of the country's old health system problems. More importantly, the solutions will be seen as most effective in the long term, once they are implemented in the short term.

Table P.1 starts off by detailing some of the major problems the U.S. has faced with its healthcare system (left column) and then suggests the current federal efforts to solve these problems (center column), followed by new solutions that are proposed (right column). Each of the chapters of this book represents a particular technological solution in which the U.S. is investing time, resources, interest, and energy.

As can be seen, the chapters that follow are grouped by theme, impact on society, and stakeholder category. Chapter 1 provides a basic theoretical foundation about the PPACA (2009) and the HITECH (Health Information Technology for Economic and Clinical Health) Act (2009) and analyzes their effect on the future of the U.S., providing descriptions of comparisons across these pieces of legislation. Chapters 2 and 3 focus on health information technology (HIT), suggesting the foundation for its uses, its value, and the necessity for an electronic framework in the U.S. Chapters 4 and 5

**Table I.1  Problems and Technological Solutions**

| Problem Faced by the United States | Current Solutions | Chapter That Explains a Potential Solution |
|---|---|---|
| A detached health system with lack of coordination and connectivity; not enough outreach in improving health literacy | Electronic government collaboration networks<br><br>Plain Writing Act<br><br>Electronic personal health records | Chapter 2: A new electronic government structure<br><br>Chapter 3: HIT (health information technology) and "Meaningful Use," policies, as well as sociocultural and environmental impacts of HIT |
| Changing individual attitudes toward health and prevention; focusing on technology that can help one understand him/herself | Mobile health apps<br><br>Video games for health improvement<br><br>Personal health records/patient controlled health records (PCHRs)<br><br>Michelle Obama's "Let's Move" Campaign<br><br>Crowdsourcing<br><br>Telemedicine | Chapter 4: Individual self-management technologies and diabetes<br><br>Chapter 5: Chronic conditions of childhood obesity, cardiovascular disease, and others |
| Government-funded prevention initiatives | HIT at CHCs (composite health care systems)<br><br>Telemedicine near disparate regions<br><br>Regional extension centers (RECs) | Chapter 6: Federal efforts for HIT at community health centers (CHCs) |
|  |  | (Continued) |

Table I.1 Problems and Technological Solutions (Continued)

| Problem Faced by the United States | Current Solutions | Chapter That Explains a Potential Solution |
|---|---|---|
| Struggles with health professionals using HIT | HIT usage at small practices—usefulness and opinions | Chapter 7: Physicians and HIT<br><br>Chapter 8: Moving forward—big data at the micro, meso, and macro levels<br><br>Cloud-based solutions |
| Community involvement: How to make prevention a community focus | Telemedicine<br><br>Regional health information organizations (RHIOs)<br><br>Regional extension centers (RECs) | Chapter 9: Geographic disparities<br><br>Chapter 10: International comparisons between the U.S. and the U.K. |
| Overview: How can these solutions be put together to make prevention a possibility? | All of the above, and more | Chapter 11: Conclusion |

take an individualized approach, asking what people can do to improve their own chances at preventing health concerns before problems arise, and producing a healthy lifestyle by supplementing health information technologies of varying kinds, including (though not limited to) mobile health apps, video games, self-management technologies, crowdsourcing, and other types of electronic health (e-health). Chapters 6 and 7 analyze what the government has done to supplement HIT efforts at various provider settings, including community health centers that affect low-income populations and small practices. The chapters include a pilot study/survey on physicians and their viewpoints on HIT. Next, Chapters 8 and 9 discuss the effects of geographic disparities and HIT at the meso, macro, and micro levels of society. Finally, Chapter 10 provides a comparative perspective, suggesting a comparison between the United States and the United Kingdom. Chapter 11 is a summary of the book, with hints about the direction that the U.S. should take toward cloud-based solutions to its electronic health infrastructure.

# About the Author

**Divya Srinivasan Sridhar** works in the field of public policy. She has developed her knowledge and experience at a number of public policy organizations including the Institute for Women's Policy Research (IWPR), National Housing Trust (NHT), Healthcare Information Management Systems Society (HIMSS), Verité Healthcare Consulting (VHC), and more. She has delved into a variety of public policy issues during her internships and graduate programs, and has published and written papers on electronic government, social policy, and healthcare, including health reform, healthcare IT, and health informatics. She completed her bachelor's degree in finance at Texas A&M University, her master's degree in public policy from the University of Texas, Dallas, specializing in social policy/health policy research, and is now working on her PhD in public policy at George Mason University in Arlington, Virginia. Srinivasan is the author of *Impact of Healthcare Informatics on Quality of Patient Care and Health Services* (CRC Press, 2013).

# INTRODUCTION

## 1

## Chapter 1

# Theoretical Underpinnings: Comparing the PPACA and HITECH Acts

## Introduction

This chapter focuses on the PPACA (Patient Protection and Affordable Care Act) and the HITECH (Health Information Technology for Economic and Clinical Health) Act, which are seen as separate entities. The author looks at a theoretical perspective on how these pieces of legislation are affecting the community, and how focused they are on prevention in public health. Also analyzed are the main players in public health, which will focus on government, the individual, the community, and physicians/health providers. This will lay the foundation for the rest of the chapters in this book, which cover these specific set of stakeholders and their importance in making prevention their purpose, and improved public health outcomes a reality. Not only can these stakeholders use the new health reform as a major pillar for change, but they also can use health information technologies as a tool for improving health, which is why these two laws and concepts should be analyzed together. This chapter's perspective is fresh, because most researchers look at what each individual legislation offers and the objectives of the legislation, rather than the bigger picture of what the legislation is proposing and whether the community is able to achieve perceived benefits. The author ties the two pieces of legislation together and analyzes similarities and differences in producing community well-being.

## Theoretical Perspectives

There are a number of theories that actually pertain to both the PPACA and the HITECH Act. These theories are a part of the Venn diagram in Figure 1.1. The way that the theories are applied and utilized by the community provide the differences in these pieces of legislation. The author begins by discussing the theories that may be used to describe both acts, and then discusses how the applications may differ when implementing and assessing the use and impact of each piece of legislation.

Health behavior theory, as suggested by Noar, Chabot, and Zimmerman (2008) as well as others, is defined as a psychological mindset of individuals to improve their own healthcare situation when provided the tools and resources to empower themselves. Global health standards and ideals as well as multiple aspects of health education and improvement ("multiples behaviors") can impact health choices and principles (Noar et al., 2008). Potential impacts from such a mindset are part of a smaller theory known as SCT, which may include the perceived susceptibility, perceived severity, perceived benefits, perceived barriers, cues to action, self-efficacy, and more, as discussed by Glanz et al., (2002). Because of the wider impact of such theory, it pertains to the PPACA and the broad ranging effects of the PPACA on the community. The health behavior

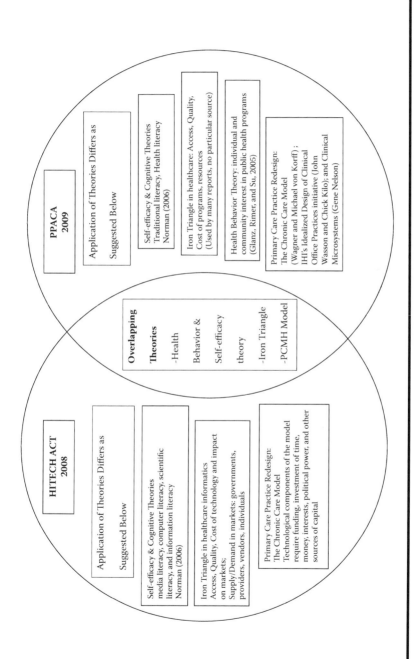

**Figure 1.1 Venn diagram: Theoretical overlap.**

theory encompasses social cognitive theory (SCT), which affects the HITECH Act of 2008.

The SCT suggests that individuals can impact their own health behaviors and goals, with a focus on literacy as the way to enrich individuals' health behaviors. To apply SCT to the HITECH Act, many of the goals of the HITECH Act include empowering individuals with new tools and technologies to provide individualized, personalized solutions to improved healthcare and introducing networks of connectivity between providers, patients/consumers, and other third party organizations. The SCT suggests a number of literacy types, with a focus on health, media, information, and computer literacy as opposed to the traditional literacy focus. The development of society through other types of technological literacy in relation to health may be where the HITECH differs from the PPACA. The HITECH Act distinctly focuses on improving individuals' computer literacy through direct and indirect initiatives. These literacy types are discussed in Chapter 2 when applied to the role of electronic government.

When applied to the PPACA, the theories may have differing outcomes than when applied to the HITECH Act.

Individuals may positively use PPACA to gain health insurance (especially those in a position to have newly acquired health insurance through expanded Medicaid coverage or subsidies on their health insurance plan), use health literacy tools provided by the government, and use preventative care strategies that are being pushed through PPACA initiatives (obesity prevention, healthier lifestyles, increase in the primary care physician workforce, and others). At the same time, some individuals may free-ride on the benefits they receive through PPACA, an option to use their newly acquired health insurance to care even less about their healthcare because it is being paid through taxpayer funds. The community has the option to not make the most out of many of the PPACA provisions that could actually benefit it. In this sense, the self-efficacy theory can really impact those who want to be impacted. Small businesses are struggling to keep afloat with the economy and the rules that now require employers to provide employee health insurance coverage. The health insurance exchange may be a way to provide new government-sponsored health coverage that can compete with private insurance companies for covering individuals. Policies against cherry-picking individuals with co-morbidities (known as "community rating" and "guaranteed issue" policies in PPACA) may have substantial impact on those who learn more about how these policies can affect them. Youth are covered under health insurance from family and guardians until the age of 26. As can be seen, the PPACA provides a set of mixed results across the community, and continues to be debated concerning its effectiveness. Much of the cost and quality effectiveness can differ based on the cognitive theory and how individuals and the community utilize the PPACA. Next is a discussion on the effects of HITECH Act using social cognitive theory (SCT).

## *Social Cognitive Theory*

The social cognitive theory can also be applied to the HITECH Act, in an applied sense, compared to the PPACA. The HITECH Act provides many provisions that make available grants, funding, and initiatives for easing technology into the provider and community settings. Yet, the impact of electronic health (e-health) is difficult to understand until it is fully utilized by the community. As will be discussed in Chapter 2, electronic government initiatives may help society learn more about their own health needs and in tracking their health behavior as well as improving the quality of their health needs. On the other hand, if providers or individuals misuse or hurt their own health outcomes by utilizing technologies, the impact is not only negative but difficult to reverse after creating a large platform for health technologies. For example, the health information exchange that involves the coordination and collaboration services for data exchange across provider settings, including hospitals, practices, and healthcare organizations (as well as business entities and other third parties that may be involved), could work to benefit providers, as well as patients who are linked to these providers. At the same time, the health information exchange may leave out many practices that cannot afford to participate (discussed in later chapters) as well as those practices or parts of the community who intentionally choose not to participate. The Health Insurance Portability and Accountability Act (HIPAA) can have positive or negative impacts on HITECH and the community, based on how cognitively useful the community finds HIPAA and whether or not the community is for or against changes to their HIPAA rights. Many of the HITECH provisions are closely entangled with the individual lifestyles of patients and consumers, and whether or not they are interested in their own healthcare and health outcomes. So again, similar to the PPACA, the benefits of HITECH may only be seen based on how much individuals are involved in their own self-efficacy.

The difference in application of the SCT and health behaviors theory may be in the degree and level to which they impact society. This stems from the health behavior theory that suggests that individuals only use tools to the extent that they believe the tools will produce effectiveness and efficiency in their lives, which is based on their level of literacy on the issues. SCT is greatly affected by health behavior theory because individuals take steps and actions to make differences in their health behaviors based on their own health literacy and how easily affected this knowledge is. While PPACA can affect traditional literacy, the HITECH Act may affect electronic and computer literacy skills that, in the big picture, will affect utilization of various health tools to impact health outcomes. Providing new means for individuals to access electronic health through pilot projects and electronic government is a step forward for the HITECH Act; if used correctly, it can improve traditional health literacy and create a strong foundation, in collaboration with the PPACA. Equipping the community with tools and legislation that suggests changes in community health is the first step toward progress. At the same time, the way that progress and outcomes are measured differs across the two pieces of legislation.

## Measuring Progress and Outcomes

The PPACA has been known to be measured through the "iron triangle" of healthcare, including the dimensions of cost, access, and quality. These three outcomes must be carefully juggled in order to produce a health system that is not too heavily focused on cost effectiveness while producing problems with quality and vice versa. Similarly, the iron triangle can be used to measure the HITECH Act outcomes, as the costs of technology can affect markets, and access to technology is affected by the digital divide (the gap between those with access to digital and IT and those without which is the result of socioeconomic barriers in society.

Both the HITECH Act and PPACA are rooted in yet another theory, known as the *Chronic Care Model*, which provides for integration of technology across healthcare settings between providers, patients, and the community. This theory illustrates the application of the health behavior theory and SCT in the real world, such that those in the community can see practical outcomes in their lives. The Chronic Care Model has four major components: the community, the health system, informed patients and families, and prepared, proactive teams. The solidarity of the four components allows for a stronger healthcare structure in the United States overall, if followed correctly. The Chronic Care Model also can address many of the disparities from geography, demographics, and the digital divide, through new creative individualized and team-based solutions. Following the Chronic Care Model is the Patient-Centered Medical Home (PCMH) movement, a practice redesign movement to restructure the objectives of the healthcare provision, specifically at health provider settings. While the overall idea is the same, the specific objectives may differ between HITECH and PPACA. The HITECH Act would advocate health information technologies in the practice, while PPACA would recommend patient-centered objectives in collaboration with HIT. (The Chronic Care Model is discussed in greater detail in Chapter 4.)

The diagram in Figure 1.1 illustrates, in a concise manner, many of the theories discussed above. Previously discussed were some of the theories to better understand the need for the PPACA and HITECH Act, and potential impacts from the two pieces of legislation. Figure 1.2 compares and contrasts health objectives of the two legislations.

A number of the objectives of the PPACA and HITECH Act are similar—the goal of the iron triangle outcomes of cost, quality care, efficiency, and more objective health measures and measurements of performance are present across both types of legislation. Priorities of the PPACA have been expanding access to health insurance with a serious amount of government expansion on many of the health decisions that were previously completed privately at the individual or health provider level. On the other hand, the HITECH Act introduces some new privacy rights for individuals (including reforms to HIPAA), as well as grants and expansion of technological infrastructure across health providers. Here, there is some level of government expansion on decision making and government access to health information that can make conservatives uncomfortable. Yet, the HITECH Act has been deemed bipartisan, though the PPACA has been accepted as left wing.

## Conclusion

This chapter highlighted some of the major theories and objectives of the PPACA and HITECH Act to provide a foundation for the next set of chapters that discuss the goal of prevention

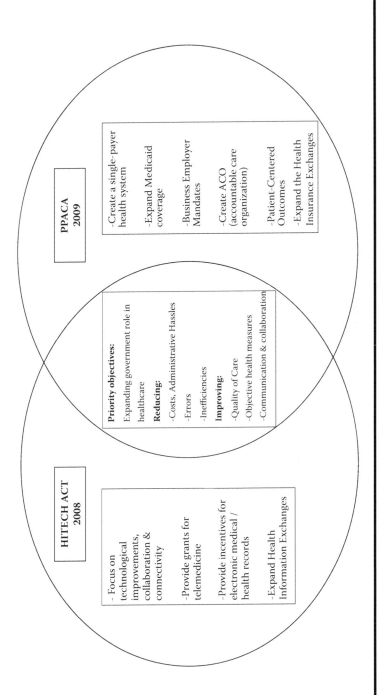

**Figure 1.2 Venn diagram of objectives.**

in healthcare. By analyzing the similarities and differences across the pieces of legislation, there is clarity as to the similar and different objectives and a reference point for the opening of a policy window for health reform issues. The U.S. government, community, and health providers can utilize these pieces of legislation as potential opportunities if they work together to overcome any problems discovered during the process.

# References

Glanz, K., Rimer, B.K. and Lewis, F.M. (eds) (2002). *Health Behavior and Health Education: Theory, Research and Practice*, 3rd edn. Jossey-Bass, San Francisco, CA.

Norman, C. D., and H. A. Skinner. 2006. eHEALS: The eHealth literacy scale. *Journal of Medical Internet Research* 8 (4), e27.

# GOVERNMENT AND TECHNOLOGY POLICIES

*Chapter 2*

# Impact of E-Government on Electronic Health Literacy

## *Chapter Summary*

The electronic information the U.S. government provides to the public on health issues may impact how the public protects itself from large-scale diseases, illnesses, and chronic conditions. These conditions may be self-inflicted or environment-based. This chapter focuses on electronic government legislation as well as past research linking survey data with electronic health knowledge and perceptions of quality, confidence, and security of information in government. The chapter first describes how the United States has made efforts in improving e-health knowledge through various pieces of e-government and e-health (as well as non-e-health) legislation. Some of these objectives are linked to the HITECH Act and PPACA legislation discussed in Chapter 1. Focus is on state and federal e-health initiatives: mobile health programs or resources, health information exchanges, and state and privately funded health information technology centers, and Regional Health Information Organizations (RHIOs). The study then applies a logistic regression on the 2007 Health Information National Trends Survey (HINTS) data analyzing the level of trust in the government that impacts interest and access to e-health data. This shows how perceptions of government and government action may impact health knowledge and access to e-health information in the community going forward.

# Introduction

As the United States goes electronic in its infrastructure, the government's electronic presence is important in improving the nation's health literacy. The reason why this is the focus of new research by electronic government is because it has impacts on society in its ability to reach a larger amount of people in a shorter period of time, while also providing a variety of messages that can improve the health outcomes of the public. It especially has become a focus in the late 2000s, from legislation discussed in the Patient Protection and Affordable Care Act (PPACA) and the Health Information Technology for Economic and Clinical Health (HITECH) Act. Through more informed interactions with government and data provided from government and nongovernment information sources, citizens can improve their awareness, education, and, most importantly, health choices and outcomes.

To better understand this subject, this chapter uses definitions from established authors of these terms and relationships and then contextualizes them for the purposes of this study. Electronic government, also known as the *virtual state* by J. Fountain (2001), is the "digitalization of data and communication [that] makes important changes to the nature, organization, and structure of government, while expanding and changing its functionalities" (p.131). Organizations express the importance of e-government by using technology to expand the reach of governmental processes in order to improve citizen participation (World Bank, 2012). This study uses this definition to support the electronic government presence through electronic health information, as well as the various reforms, legislations, and initiatives that have been in favor of moving health onto an electronic platform. The focus is primarily on a government to citizen, (G2C), framework rather than the government to government (G2G) or government to business (G2B) models. To provide a better context of the e-government initiatives that affect electronic health (e-health) outcomes, following is a discussion of the definition of e-health.

E-health, used in a scientific context, is "an emerging field in the intersection of medical informatics, public health, and business, referring to health services and information delivered or enhanced through the Internet and related technologies" (Fountain, 2001, p.130). Thus, e-health literacy is the extension of this definition, representing how citizens interact with the health information available in electronic sources to find, understand, and apply knowledge gained to solve their health problems. The author's study defines electronic health literacy as the level of awareness that the individuals in a region have toward the resources, opportunities, education, and knowledge of health issues occurring around them in a digital format and in any given time frame. These two fields, e-health and e-government, have been seen to interact and impact each other in important ways. This chapter explores a variety of different concepts within e-health and e-government. The following are the objectives of the chapter:

1. The first objective of the chapter is to identify U.S. legislation that directly or indirectly impacts electronic health literacy for the community. This includes various parts

of the health reform act, such as the PPACA and Health Insurance Portability and Accountability Act (HIPAA), the development of the health information exchanges (HIEs), RHIOs for infrastructure improvements, the Plain Writing Act, and other important pieces of government legislation.

2. Then, the study provides a policy analysis of how these electronic government initiatives and legislation impact both health and e-health literacy, albeit in direct or indirect ways, such as through improving funding, information asymmetry problems, outreach, or other reasons.

3. The next objective of the chapter is to see what relationships are present between public trust, confidence, and perceptions of safety in health information and the public's confidence in health information from various health information sources: the media, government, Internet, e-government, and charities. The independent variable (confidence in each of these sources of information) is hypothesized to have effects on three dependent variables: security of information, confidence in government information, and concern for quality of care in health information. Using the relationships found, it could be presumed that sources of information can improve e-health literacy and quality of care perceptions for the public.

Some of the e-health legislation and initiatives by government will have short-term policy consequences, while others have long-term ones. Because this chapter has a primary focus on e-health literacy through improvements to quality of care, information security, and confidence in information sources for individuals with chronic conditions, the secondary focus is on reducing the digital divide. This digital divide encompasses individuals (typically of disadvantaged or low-income backgrounds), who are unable to participate in activities that involve technologies due to cost, access, and/or ignorance. By receiving access to health technologies, they may gain new avenues for treating health and chronic conditions, but many a time, even with exposure to new technologies, they may face lack of interest in the technologies or lack of emotional and educational support in using the technologies to their fullest capacity. The digital divide is a difficult concept to measure, and for the purposes of this study it is primarily measured by using variables that control for income and socioeconomic status, even though these are not the only variables that represent the digital divide. Also pointed out in this chapter is legislation that best represents the digital divide, including the Plain Writing Act.

Tertiary focuses of the paper include: the ethical implications of an electronic health environment; interactions between state, federal, and local agencies through the process; and impacts of the e-health information retrieval for the community.

## Theory

The discussion first provides theory on e-health literacy and its presence in various communities. This literature will provide the foundation for the study on improving e-health literacy for individuals with chronic conditions.

Norman and Skinner (2006) discuss some of the foundations of the e-health literacy concepts, rooted in social cognitive theory (SCT), which suggests the importance of competencies and confidence for individuals and communities to develop health awareness and skill development. In this context, the "skills" researchers speak of would be acquiring new health information to treat chronic conditions, such as cancer. Social cognitive theory is particularly useful in communication of health objectives, because it incorporates the environmental, personal, and behavioral factors involved in producing behavioral change. For an individual, self-efficacy (a feeling of self-reliance in one's decisions) is important, while collective efficacy is important for communities in understanding concepts about health from their peers. Behavioral learning is an important concept because individuals and communities can react to health information if they are aware of the behavior and feel they have the potential to act (Bandura, 2004). Thus, the concept of behavioral learning is tested through the methods section of this chapter. SCT provides a strong theoretical foundation for e-health literacy because testing how the public perceives health information from an e-government can be important to whether or not they find confidence and trust in health information as well as concern for quality of care.

There has been discussion on e-health literacy and how technology plays a role in its growth. Norman and Skinner (2006) also discuss different cases where health practitioners can address e-health knowledge issues in clinical or public health practice through six literacy types: traditional, health, media, computer, scientific, and information. A literate environment for public health is created by an environment of patient care, preventive medicine and health promotion, population-level health communication campaigns, and health professionals' research and practical work, which is evaluated in its applicability to consumer health informatics (Bandura, 2004). Many of these environments can be, and are being, created by governments in improving understanding of health, as discussed in the next section—government legislation and initiatives. The author tests only Norman and Skinner's information literacy component, which is defined as usage, applicability, and awareness of health information. These three information literacy components will be encompassed in the variables tested in the study.

Another study by Davis et al. (2002) suggests the importance of health literacy work on cancer outcomes. Through the improvement of risk communication and informed consent of healthcare resources and programs, many obstacles that cancer patients currently face in accessing and utilizing health information may be removed. An important point to be noted by the authors is the disparity between disadvantaged and more advantaged cancer patients, because disadvantaged individuals lack the opportunities and interest to use health information, which may hinder their ability to prevent, assess, or find treatments and recommendations for their conditions. This, in turn, puts a heavier burden on the healthcare system. Another point to be noted is that an individual's health literacy can be less adequate than his/her overall knowledge. The authors suggest that disparities may impact the attitudes of lower-income individuals who are seeking help for their health condition. The author's study builds on these theories, and takes this one step farther, by analyzing health literacy outcomes affected by e-government, by presenting various pieces of legislation that are trying to reduce the disparities that exist between different socioeconomic groups, which is discussed next.

## Sources of E-Health Initiatives by E-Government

The following are some ways that support how government, especially e-government, may be impacting the concern for quality of health information, security, and confidence of health facts. These initiatives and various government legislation may be driving some of the conclusions in a study on cancer patients.

### Mobile Health Initiatives

A number of reports analyze how mobile initiatives led by governments can have an impact on the community (Kennedy (2005), Koontz (2004), and Kules and Xie (2011)). The Mobile Government 2010 and Beyond Report, funded by the European Union Regional Development Fund, discusses how electronic and mobile sources of government has spread public health awareness messages to the world, including in both developed and developing parts of the world (Rannu, Saksing, and Mahlakoiv, 2010). This report could especially impact how cancer patients use health information to help them handle their chronic condition (Rannu, Saksing, and Mahlakoiv, 2010). These resources can be prescription reminders, tips about healthy behaviors for specific conditions, such as pregnancy (Maternal Health Initiative Text 4 Health), health professional's education, disease alerts, emergency messages, and humanitarian aid alerts.

Vital Wave Consulting (2009) published a report discussing mobile health technologies and their impact on the developing world. While the western world has mainly used the mobile health devices for training of its healthcare professionals, the eastern world has caught on to mobile health (m-health) trends for a variety of purposes: education and awareness, remote data collection, remote monitoring, communication and training for healthcare workers, disease and epidemic outbreak tracking, diagnostic and treatment support, and more. The report also suggests that "SMS (short message service) alerts have a measurable impact on, and a greater ability to, influence behavior than radio and television campaigns" (p. 12). This would be an interesting hypothesis to test and add to the methods of this chapter. Trust in the media was tested on e-health literacy outcomes, though it did not generate statistical significance in this study, but the case of SMS and mobile texts could have a significant outcome on health literacy.

## Initiatives to Reduce the Digital Divide

An article by West and Miller (2006) discusses the indirect relationship between increasing perceptions of information security, trust in health information, and trust in electronic government, with lower levels of educational background and lower income. These populations, typically of lower classes, are the most susceptible and trusting of government security and accessibility to information. West and Miller discuss steps that U.S. state health departments and state agencies have taken in reaching the public, especially populations with disadvantaged backgrounds. One step toward closing this "digital divide," where these populations don't have access to e-health, has been public e-health initiatives to "reduce regional variation in accessibility, privacy, and security" (pp. 652–666). Some states that performed well in this aspect, especially introducing variation in e-government, include Massachusetts, Texas, Indiana, Tennessee, California, Michigan, Pennsylvania, New York, and Kentucky.

Brodie et al. (2000) analyzed results of two surveys that were conducted with an oversampling of African American adults and children, relative to disparate populations. The surveys discussed general electronic information literacy and also had more specific health literacy questions (pp. 255–265). It took a look at opinions of the public and reactions to government interventions to provide e-health, and found that 57% of those surveyed think government interventions are likely to impact the low-income population and those digitally divided. It also looked at government transactions with health-related government agencies across race, ethnicity, and other socio-economic variables, and found that government will have a harder time reaching such uneven groups. There are particular features of importance to specific races, such as privacy to African Americans and portability to other races. These individual differences in preference of mode of communication for various demographic groups may impact whether e-government impinges more on one group than another.

## Legislation Impacting E-Health Literacy

Authors have discussed the importance and growth in an electronic government (e-government) infrastructure, but literature does not explore how the presence of e-government impacts and facilitates the presence of community health outcomes and electronic health (e-health) literacy, especially for those with chronic conditions. The focus on one chronic condition, cancer, in this study is purposeful because it has weighed down on the United States as an expensive condition that impacts the wallets of the government and society, while also greatly impacting quality of life and living conditions for those individuals with the disease. It seems logical that e-government would want to reach cancer patients who have the greatest health risks and may be impacted significantly in their health outcomes from e-government presence and communication.

Here lies the focus of this section: To determine to what extent the U.S. government impacts electronic health initiatives through important legislation that incorporates federal and state funding and nonfunding initiatives. The presence of important legislation is discussed, because this creates the foundation for e-health improvements by e-government. The literature is grouped into two categories: legislation directly impacting e-health and legislation impacting non-e-health initiatives (but still indirectly impacting community health).

## Key Legislation for Furthering E-Health

There are a number of important factors that impact government action: confidence in government information, trust in the security of e-government information, and concern for quality of care. These relationships between e-government sources of e-health information and trust, confidence, and security may be strengthened or weakened based on how successful efforts are to uphold various government legislation. The following are examples of legislation that have an impact on security, privacy, and confidence in e-government: Health Insurance Portability and Accountability Act (HIPAA), the Genetic Information Nondiscrimination Act (GINA) 2008, mobile health technology initiatives, the Health Information Exchanges (HIEs) and Regional Health Information Organizations (RHIOs). These will be discussed in greater detail to show how government is working toward the goals of security, privacy, transparency, quality, and confidence.

The author's survey analysis was limited in its scope of information sources, as there were no variables for the newest set of initiatives that government has focused on—mobile health technologies. These include any handheld devices and/ or mobile devices—phones, tablets, laptop computers, and more—through which the government can communicate health information to individuals.

Looking specifically at legislation and policy initiatives embracing mobile health technologies, there are several provisions of the American Recovery and Reinvestment Act (ARRA) that support an e-health and mobile-health (m-health) infrastructure. An important provision of the ARRA in favor of health information technologies (HITs) and mobile health is the HITECH Act of 2009. The HITECH Act devotes resources specifically to development of a high technology infrastructure in healthcare through the use of electronic health records, telemedicine, research on the growing use of mobile health technologies, and more discussed in Chapter 1. These techniques, especially the use of m-health technologies, are prevalent in many developing and developed nations today.

Other legislation impacts the level of confidence in government information, especially new changes to security and privacy guidelines. During health reform, the passage of the Patient Protection and Affordable Care Act (PPACA) links to many of the same outcomes as the HITECH Act. The PPACA was an important health reform legislation that introduced numerous HIT regulations, including the HIPAA Rule with privacy guidelines for health providers, development of health insurance exchanges, and grant funding for EMRs. HIPAA could be a reason for much scrutiny by providers, and greater anxiety and skepticism by individuals on how their electronic records are being maintained. While the HITECH Act is not officially part of or connected to the PPACA, the development of its goals and entities were accomplished along the same lines.

Chronic diseases are especially sensitive because of the way insurance companies, employers, and providers view these conditions. Due to how expensive they are, insurance companies shy away from having to cover these costs, thus impacting employers who find it expensive to hire those with such preexisting conditions. These problems of discrimination have led to the introduction of important health reform provisions, such as a community rating and guaranteed provision. These have stated that insurance companies will no longer be allowed to discriminate on the grounds of preexisting conditions. Along the same lines, GINA also was introduced to provide safety and security of patients' genetic information, accessibility to physicians, providers, insurance companies, etc. GINA can have important ripple effects across the community because such genetic information could be used against individuals during employment, for discrimination and prejudice that could harm one's safety, and for adverse selection purposes by health insurance companies.

Because these pieces of legislation concern similar and overlapping subject matter, these Acts work together in solving many issues in HIT reform. The PPACA impacts mobile health technologies through HIPAA, which lead to changes in security standards of m-health technologies, perceived by the community. GINA and HIPAA together form the pillars for improving the safeguarding of e-health information across providers. They also work to ensure that unfair access to confidential and sensitive information does not occur through the presence of PHIs (personal health information) or personal health identifiers that replace individuals' names in large health datasets.

## Health Insurance Exchanges

The development of health information exchanges is an important e-health initiative headed by e-government in the United States. The National E-Health Collaborative published a report on ways to create national standards for information on the Internet to improve patient care and cut costs more efficiently. Some examples of such HIEs include a roadmap to include the

Care Connectivity Consortium, HealthBridge, Indiana Health Information Exchange, Inland Northwest Services, and Kaiser Permanente. These organizations place emphasis on the following: "... focus on the patient, build trust with stakeholders and exchange partners, bring value to the participants, be flexible and responsive to community needs" (p. 5). All of these support the major factors that individuals with chronic conditions see as important, as discussed in this study.

GE Healthcare in 2010 developed a white paper on the subject of the HIEs, discussing the benefits and challenges to development of the HIEs. Some examples include environmental benefits, cost-cutting abilities, information transparency, difficulties in development of standards of commitment, and more.

Yet, much of the literature does not discuss the development of an electronic and transparent portal of information with comparisons of health plans in the health insurance market, which is the purpose of the HIE. The federal and state guidance on HIPAA is not clear as to how it will impact the HIEs, because HIEs are external sources of data rather than internal sources like a physician's office or electronic HIT vendor. This is another unknown with the creation of the HIEs that could have impacts on the community and its understanding, acceptance, and access of/to e-health information.

# RHIOs

Regional Health Information Organizations (RHIOs) are similar to HIEs, but take on both public sector and private funding to reach their goals of being technologically driven and connected. They provide a forum for hospitals and/or physicians to access and store their patient's data and connect to an EMR (electronic medical record) system. Data may be centrally monitored and secured by other private companies or public sector organizations that have security. The RHIOs are an intermediary between the healthcare provider, the patient, and EMR vendors, as well as state and local governments that may be involved in these initiatives. For this reason, RHIOs serve an important purpose in furthering electronic medical record usage, as well as facilitating use of federal and state funding toward improved technology usage. It works as an intermediary to e-government in furthering the efforts to improve the e-health infrastructure of the nation.

An example of a state-based RHIO includes: MedVirginia. The VA (the Veterans Affairs) Department has started a pilot to share patient records between the Richmond VA Medical Center and MedVirginia, which expands the virtual lifetime electronic record (VLER) program across a state and federal entity. On the other hand, an example of a federally funded RHIO is The Total Health Record of Wyoming (THR), which is supported by government funding. The THR network, local networks, and the WyHIE network will work together to support exchange of healthcare information across Wyoming and the region.

Patient information is stored by various partners and audited by various organizations to ensure privacy and security is upheld. The implementation and use of this intermediary, which has control over information security for patients, is an important and daunting task.

Next the author looks at other types of government initiatives through electronic means.

## Web Design and E-Health

Other government and state agencies discuss the use of modern tools and technologies including Web design and search engine optimization, and its importance to the government in delivering services to mobile and nonmobile electronic devices. Optimizing content with an interface that is user friendly, rather than "just translating content from paper-based documents to the Web," will facilitate in the spread of information, as demonstrated by numerous government health and nonhealth Web sites and applications with new interfaces.* The interfaces tend to provide tools with multimedia and video, educational resources, datasets, and health calculators, to list a few. These interfaces serve different audiences and provide information to all age groups and for specific, as well as general, health information. Government agencies will need to keep current with the latest design concepts and refresh content delivery mechanisms for higher quality and performance standards. The government has created the Digital Services Advisory Group for this purpose.

The presence of high-quality, highly "usable" Web sites also may be a step in the direction of improving e-health literacy, as discussed by the Centers for Disease Control and Prevention (CDC).† Usability has two components that the CDC defines as (1) "a quality attribute of 'user interfaces,' or the part of a product that a person interacts with;" and (2) "a method to make it easier for end users to complete tasks."

Mobile technologies provide opportunities for public health outreach and improvements in the "health, safety, and preparedness" of the United States and other nations. There are three main components that distinguish mobile health technology from nonmobile technology: portability, affordability, and availability, which make health information and collecting disease/health data efficient and effective (Centers for Disease Control and Prevention, 2010). There are three main forms of mobile health tools that the CDC defines, including downloadable apps, mobile Web sites, and texts (CDC Media Toolkit). None of these were available in the dataset that was tested, but it would make for an important improvement in the study to focus on the mobile health component to cancer patients' e-health usage.

---

* Online at: http://www.womenshealth.gov/; http://www.healthcare.gov/; http://www.cdc.gov/; http://www.census.gov

† Online at: http://blogs.cdc.gov/healthliteracy/2012/07/17/why-usability-matters-to-health-literacy/

## Non-Health-Related Legislation Furthering E-Health

As the author's study will show through survey research and analysis, individuals most trusting in e-government data tend to be of lower income backgrounds, tend to have poorer overall health, tend to have more stress, and many are from specific geographic settings. This means that e-health reaches some more than others, and e-health literacy may be improved only if these populations are more aware of e-government and e-health resources, problems, and impacts.

Transparency in government writing, grants, funding, and programs will improve the speed and efficiency with which information reaches the public, as the Plain Writing Act, H.R. 946, suggests. This is especially true for lower income and less educated classes that currently do not make use of the resources that are actually available to them, due to either ignorance or a perception of what the programs do or require. This act could have positive impacts on the transparency of health information and improve access to information regarding health insurance, preventive healthcare, and free and low-cost prescription drug resources, which are some of the basic needs of U.S. residents that are to be addressed. Some of these potential outcomes are stated in the goals of the Public Health Service Act (PHSA), part of the newly published rules of the PPACA* to reduce discrimination and improve access to health-care for all. Typically, the writing in such rules is verbose and hard to comprehend, especially for the average layman. The Plain Writing Act, H.R. 946, introduced in October 2010, is an important foundation for all e-health literacy initiatives by the government, because reaching low-income populations can be facilitated by the use of plain, clear language in all

---

* Section 2713 of the Public Health Service Act ("PHSA"), as added by the Patient Protection and Affordable Care Act ("PPACA" or the "Act"), generally requires that group health plans and insurers offering group or individual health insurance: (1) provide coverage for certain preventive health services, and (2) not impose cost-sharing requirements with respect to such services.

government acts. This act, in turn, will improve health literacy and also possibly support better health outcomes in the future.

Community views and opinions on the level and strength of coordination between e-governments at different levels of government (local, state, federal) and of different countries was not present in the study, but could be a valuable addition, as noted by the goals of "Benefits of President's E-Government Initiatives of 2012," a report to Congress.* The report does an analysis of funding initiatives for e-governance in the Department of Health and Human Services (DHHS) through a Government to Citizen Portfolio. The report discusses expanding various committees and their lines of business (LoB): Budget Formulation and Execution LoB, Federal Health Architecture LoB, Financial Management LoB, Geospatial LoB, and more, to provide assistance with funding for electronic invoicing, documenting, Web portals, and health initiatives to enhance an electronic infrastructure for U.S. residents. The report provides good strategies for health programs that need to improve their electronic infrastructure and also state what the executive is doing to improve e-health for the nation. The opportunity to use Web portals, e-invoicing, and e-documents may improve communication and coordination between government or nongovernment health agencies and between health and nonhealth agencies, which will improve the overall status of e-health for the public.

A GAO (Government Accountability Office) report on e-government initiatives, sponsored by the Office of Management and Budget, discusses how different e-government strategies have had a mixed response by both the public and private agencies, something that was explored in this study. As seen in the author's study, health information from charities was widely used by low-income populations and seemed to be the only type of information that impacts concern for quality of

---

* Online at http://whitehouse.gov/sites/default/files/omb/assets/egov_fy12_e-gov_benefits_report.pdf

health information. This could be because those who get their information from charities think the quality of the information is sound, or because they have no other choice in access to health information. For this reason, initiatives like this, through funding new programs and providing correct information and resources to the public through both public and private information sources, is important. The creation of committees or audit control bodies that test whether the information being provided is accurate is of great importance because the public is relying on it.

## Policy Analysis: Summary of Importance of E-Government on E-Health Literacy

Table 2.1 is a summary of direct and indirect initiatives for the public for the growing use of e-government tactics for chronic condition prevention and treatment.

### Trust in Information Sources and Impacts on E-Health Literacy Outcomes

This portion of the chapter uses statistical analysis to test how Americans with cancer, a chronic disease, use electronic health data and how they perceive e-government. The main variable being studied is trust in various sources of information: trust from government, e-government, the Internet, charities, and other organizations. The objective of the study is to figure out whether trust in e-government impacts various factors: perception of quality of healthcare, safety of health information, and level of confidence in health information. So, the null hypothesis predicts that trust in e-government will not (1) increase concern for quality of care, (2) improve perceptions of secure information, and (3) improve confidence in health information. The alpha hypothesis suggests that a direct

**Table 2.1   Policy Analysis of e-Government Initiatives**

| Direct E-Health Initiatives | Consequence |
| --- | --- |
| Better Web sites, user interface, online communication tools | Providing transparent information for prevention, awareness<br><br>Provide better information retrieval, access, productivity |
| HIPAA and GINA | Can very much affect how HIEs are formed, facilitated, and improved; they also may impact the kind and quality of information floating around with regards to privacy, security of information on the Internet and access to confidential information through regulation and penalties for lawbreakers |
| Mobile health: Definition and use may differ among developed and developing countries | Created new ways to reach the public, data mining through social networking, reaching populations with mobile phones and mobile devices |
| E-health literacy workshops, training, programs to serve communities | Focuses on e-health literacy, changes to quality of care standards, and reduces digital divide |
| Indirect Initiatives | Consequences |
| Creation and collaboration with RHIOs | Some state-funded RHIOs and government organizations that work with RHIOs can improve the efficiency in health outcomes for hospitals with this technology |
| Building HIEs and other tools/resources for low-income populations to better equip them with e-health information | Addresses the digital divide, improves information asymmetry |
| U.S. HITECH Act, ARRA funding | Has helped build new structures and funding for audit, quality control, information management, and collaboration |

relationship may exist between trust in government and these three dependent variables.

## Methods

Using a logistic regression from HINTS 2007 data, an analysis of the survey results showed how the public accesses health information and how interested the community is in its health outcomes. Relationships were found to exist between various health literacy outcomes and e-government as well as demographic factors that may be impacting these outcomes. The dependent variables were (1) trust in health information, (2) concern for quality of health information, and (3) concern for information safety. The idea was to test how various government and nongovernmental independent variables (sources of information: Internet, government, e-government, media, and charitable organizations, age, education, and other factors) impact how health information is perceived by the public. This tackles e-health literacy from the standpoint of interest and value in health information by analyzing how concerned the public is about the information they use.

### New Contribution to the Field: New E-Government Term

The HINTS dataset has been analyzed by other authors, but so far there has not been emphasis on an e-government variable. This variable was defined as the impact of an e-government infrastructure, created through an interaction term, statistically calculated by combining the trust in Internet and trust in government variable. This will be the foundation of the results of the study—to analyze whether e-government impacts the concern for quality, safeguards, and trust in health-related information by individuals in the community. Based on whether or not this variable is significant, there will be a policy analysis of next steps and how to improve the engagement of e-government in improving the community's perception of health information and interest in accessing it. The trust in information provided by e-government is a proxy for trust in e-government. Thus, results are in the format as the trust in e-government increases/ decreases, the Y variable increases by X.XX percent.

Table 2.2 through Table 2.4 provide results on the important factors impacting e-health literacy outcomes.

Table 2.2 analyzes the concern the community has about health information. This table demonstrates that some variables do affect the concern for health information. The variables with statistical significance include: trust in the Internet, the level of confidence individuals have in getting health information, the location of the individuals (division they are in), and individuals' level of stress. These variables impact how concerned individuals are about the quality of their health information. For example, with more trust in the Internet, the individuals will be about 32% less likely to be concerned about their health information. Similarly, with greater confidence in health information, there is less concern about the quality of health information found. Yet, when individuals are undergoing higher levels of stress, they are more likely to care about the type of health information they find, potentially because of the correlation between stress and other health conditions. These individuals were cancer patients, making it important to study what affects their concern for health information. On the other hand, the level of trust in e-government and government health agencies was not actually significant in impacting those individuals' concerns about their health information. Considering the results that trust in the Internet makes individuals less worried about the accuracy and quality of their health information suggests that e-health literacy needs to be a major goal of the government and the community. Improving the information presented in online forums and on

**Table 2.2 Concern for Quality of Health Information Retrieved**

| Number of observations = | 570.00 | | | | | |
|---|---|---|---|---|---|---|
| LR chi2(11) = | 52.42 | | | | | |
| Prob > chi2 = | 0.00 | | | | | |
| Pseudo R2 = | 0.07 | | | | | |
| *Concern about Quality of Health Information* | *Odds Ratio* | *Std. Error* | *z* | *P > z* | *95% Confidence Interval* | |
| Trust in Internet | 0.68[a] | 0.14 | −1.80 | 0.07 | 0.45 | 1.03 |
| Confidence about health | 0.44[b] | 0.08 | −4.49 | 0.00 | 0.31 | 0.63 |
| Perceived information safety | 0.96 | 0.31 | −0.14 | 0.89 | 0.51 | 1.80 |
| Division | 0.78[c] | 0.10 | −2.01 | 0.04 | 0.62 | 0.99 |
| Region | 1.64 | 0.49 | 1.65 | 0.10 | 0.91 | 2.94 |
| Age | 1.00 | 0.00 | 0.82 | 0.41 | 1.00 | 1.00 |
| BMI (base mass index) | 1.00 | 0.00 | 0.03 | 0.98 | 1.00 | 1.00 |
| Level of stress | 3.42[b] | 1.52 | 2.76 | 0.01 | 1.43 | 8.18 |
| Education | 0.87 | 0.09 | −1.25 | 0.21 | 0.71 | 1.08 |
| General health | 0.93 | 0.09 | −0.79 | 0.43 | 0.77 | 1.12 |
| Gender | 0.79 | 0.14 | −1.32 | 0.19 | 0.55 | 1.12 |

[a] $p < 0.10$
[b] $p < 0.01$
[c] $p < 0.05$

the Web is going to become very influential in impacting the communities' retrieval of health information. The results are shown in Table 2.2.

The next variables that are explored are the ones that impact the communities' perception that their information is

**Table 2.3    Perception that Information Is Safely Guarded**

| Number of obs = | 570 | | | | | |
|---|---|---|---|---|---|---|
| LR chi2(11) = | 25.16 | | | | | |
| Prob > chi2 = | 0.0087 | | | | | |
| Log likelihood = | −154.49022 | | | | | |
| Pseudo R2 = | 0.0753 | | | | | |
| *Information Given Doctors Is Safely Guarded* | *Odds Ratio* | *Std. Error* | *z* | *P > z* | *95% Confidence Interval* | |
| Confident about health | 1.57 | 0.52 | 1.37 | 0.17 | 0.82 | 3.00 |
| Concern for information quality | 1.05 | 0.16 | 0.29 | 0.77 | 0.77 | 1.41 |
| E-government interaction term | 1.80[a] | 0.58 | 1.84 | 0.07 | 0.96 | 3.38 |
| Division | 1.24 | 0.26 | 1.03 | 0.31 | 0.82 | 1.87 |
| Region | 0.57 | 0.30 | −1.09 | 0.28 | 0.20 | 1.57 |
| Age | 1.01 | 0.01 | 1.31 | 0.19 | 0.99 | 1.03 |
| BMI (base mass index) | 1.00 | 0.00 | −0.37 | 0.71 | 1.00 | 1.00 |
| Stress level | 1.10 | 0.42 | 0.25 | 0.80 | 0.52 | 2.31 |
| Education | 0.63[b] | 0.13 | −2.31 | 0.02 | 0.43 | 0.93 |
| General health | 0.66[c] | 0.10 | −2.65 | 0.01 | 0.48 | 0.90 |
| Gender | 0.54[a] | 0.19 | −1.72 | 0.09 | 0.27 | 1.09 |

[a]  $p < 0.10$
[b]  $p < 0.05$
[c]  $p < 0.01$

**Table 2.4    Level of Confidence in Getting Health Information**

| Number of obs = | 570 | | | | | |
|---|---|---|---|---|---|---|
| LR chi2(13) = | 62.82 | | | | | |
| Prob > chi2 = | 0.00 | | | | | |
| Log likelihood = | −351.38166 | | | | | |
| Pseudo R2 = | 0.0821 | | | | | |
| *Confident about Health* | *Odds Ratio* | *Std. Error* | *z* | *P > z* | *95% Confidence Interval* | |
| Trust in e-government interaction term[a] | 2.00[a] | 0.41 | 3.36 | 0.00 | 1.34 | 3.00 |
| Concerned about health[b] | 0.44[a] | 0.08 | −4.41 | 0.00 | 0.31 | 0.63 |
| Information safety | 1.65 | 0.53 | 1.55 | 0.12 | 0.88 | 3.09 |
| Trust in the media | 0.85 | 0.17 | −0.80 | 0.43 | 0.57 | 1.26 |
| Trust in charities | 1.10 | 0.22 | 0.51 | 0.61 | 0.75 | 1.62 |
| Division | 1.02 | 0.13 | 0.18 | 0.85 | 0.80 | 1.31 |
| Region | 1.02 | 0.31 | 0.06 | 0.95 | 0.56 | 1.86 |
| Age | 1.00 | 0.00 | 0.38 | 0.71 | 1.00 | 1.00 |
| BMI (base mass index) | 1.00 | 0.00 | −0.10 | 0.92 | 1.00 | 1.00 |
| Stress level | 0.50[b] | 0.20 | −1.71 | 0.09 | 0.22 | 1.11 |
| Education | 1.14 | 0.13 | 1.16 | 0.24 | 0.92 | 1.41 |
| General health | 0.87 | 0.08 | −1.45 | 0.15 | 0.72 | 1.05 |
| Gender | 1.08 | 0.20 | 0.40 | 0.69 | 0.74 | 1.57 |

[a] $p < 0.01$
[b] $p < 0.10$

being safeguarded by their health provider. It is again interesting to study whether or how trust in e-government impacts the trust in the health provider and how secure one feels about his/her health information. As later chapters suggest, big data and online health records are causing an uproar on how safe and secure is electronic health information stored in doctors' offices.

Table 2.3 suggests that the factors that most impact a perception of safely guarded data include trust in e-government, educational background, general health, and gender. Results suggest that the higher the level of trust in e-government, there is an 80% higher likelihood of a perception that information is being safely guarded by health providers. This could be because the greater the knowledge and interest of the community in the PPACA, new health reform issues, HIPAA, and other government and e-government initiatives, the more likely the community is to understand what their provider is doing with their health information and how it is being stored. The educational background variable suggests that greater education causes greater fear and concern about how information is safeguarded. The better that one's general health, the less the concern is for safeguarded data. Finally, for a female, it is less likely to impact security of information. Table 2.3 shows the results of the analysis.

The last variable studied was how confident individuals felt about accessing health information, and to see the relevance in e-government in the retrieval of health information (Table 2.4). The level of confidence in accessing health information was significantly impacted by trust in e-government, concern for quality of health information, and general level of stress. The greater the trust in e-government there was nearly a 200% higher level, or 2 times the original level, of confidence in accessing health information. The less the stress level, the greater the confidence in health information. Finally, the less the concern about quality of health information, the greater the confidence in health information. Table 2.4 demonstrates factors impacting trust in health information.

## Interpretation and Results

The null hypothesis for the study was that e-government has no impact on the concern, quality of, safety for, and confidence in the health information. Rejecting the null hypothesis would suggest that e-government has a role (direct or indirect) in impacting the type of information gathered by the patients in the study. The study fails to reject the null hypothesis on the variable "concern for quality of health information." This factor was not impacted by e-government, and had an inverse relationship between trust in the Internet and confidence in e-government health. On the other hand, the null hypothesis was successfully rejected for the other two dependent variables: perceived safeguarding of information and confidence in one's health information.

The following is a summary of all of the results from the study:

1. With increasing trust in e-government, there was increasing confidence in health information by survey respondents.
2. With increasing trust in e-government, there was a higher likelihood that information in provider settings was perceived as being safeguarded and secure.
3. Trust in e-government did not impact concern for quality of health information. Yet, trust in the Internet did affect the concern for higher quality health information, suggesting that electronic modes of communication are becoming more important. Other variables, such as confidence in one's health and level of stress affected the concern for quality health information.

Many of these results above seem logical. Factors, such as socioeconomic status, education, and background, may impact access and interest in health information in various settings and to varying levels. Access and interest in health information, especially from electronic means, translates to impacts on e-health literacy. The trust in government and electronic government, though not always significant, does seem to be a factor in how confident and satisfied the public is in the health information received.

Looking carefully at what e-government has done in providing direct and indirect health policy initiatives also may fortify some of these results through improved security and safeguards, or the inability to improvise on quality of health information using a digital infrastructure centered around patients and the public.

There is no way to know whether cancer patients act differently from other patients because this study only measures cancer patients' perceptions. Yet, based on the results found, it is possible that individuals with other chronic conditions have similar attitudes toward e-government in this study. The retrieval of the health information process may be impacted by trust in e-government. Cancer patients are an important set of respondents to test because it is possible that they take an active part in regulating their condition or getting help in regulating their condition.

The last part of this chapter will suggest policy recommendations on the subject of e-government and health information usage.

## Policy Recommendations and Conclusions

Policy recommendations stem from the following basic principles that can provide a strong electronic government structure for countries to support themselves as well as interact with each other on a global scale. The author suggests that e-government become (1) more information centric, (2) have a shared platform, (3) be customer centric, and (4) have privacy/security-enabling features when distributing health information.

The analysis of various government legislation and the study on cancer patients suggests that trust in e-government can have an impact on the decisions individuals make about their own health. They are using new electronic modes of information to retrieve news and updates on health, and improving the condition of information on the Internet may improve concerns they originally held with the type of health information present. A stronger e-government that has a documented purpose for e-health and initiatives toward improved e-health literacy can affect how secure individuals believe their information is, and the confidence they have in their own health.

Other recommendations are suggested by the author to get a better sense of the community's interest and views on health and e-government. There is a need for more pilot projects that evaluate how lower-income populations may use technology to receive health information, and whether it has any impact on them. These populations tend to have the greatest need for preventive healthcare and have the highest rates of emergency room usage, which can be expensive and draining on the government budget. If no such effect seems to be impacting this community (as the mobile technology usage has not penetrated to this level for socioeconomic reasons), there may be a need to reach these populations in traditional ways. Foregoing paper-based and brick-and-mortar health information locations could prove unsafe and unfair to populations that lack access, as shown by how trusting these populations tend to be in information from free and charitable organizations.

E-health and e-government may impact certain parts of the world and parts of a country faster than others. This can be typical of many types of regulations, especially as some countries face peaks in their technology adoption and integration. The idea is that e-health technology platforms should have some basic features in common (be compatible) to drive the best results, coordination, and collaboration efforts between e-health resources and e-government legislation and initiatives.

Increasing collaboration is a key policy goal for the short and long term. This collaboration is required between direct and indirect state and federal initiatives to improve efficiency and reduce waste of similarly oriented technology programs and Web portals. Some examples of direct initiatives are the creation of Web sites for the state that are linked to the federal sites, such that there is no duplication of irrelevant information or the presence of incorrect information. Some of these sites should have links to health resources. Collaboration is especially important in the creation of the health information exchange, which directly impacts the public in its choice of health insurance policies. Indirect initiatives may include funding for programs, such as RHIOS, that have a role in laying out the infrastructure for citizens.

Security and privacy are important concerns for federal, state, local, and individual health data that is extremely sensitive in nature. For this reason, the presence of legislation (such as HIPAA) about privacy and security regulation (and penalties for lack thereof) as well as the actual bodies of regulations (auditing agencies and organizations) will play an important role in secure data storage, access, and warehousing going forward.

E-health initiatives are, and will, continue to impact the market for skilled healthcare professionals with capabilities to mine "big" data,* individuals trained in healthcare IT, and maintenance and audit of quality control programs for the data and the technological systems. This will ensure their presence

---

* Big data is high-volume, high-velocity, and high-variety information assets that demand cost-effective, innovative forms of information processing for enhanced insight and decision making.

is continually updated and that it remains cutting edge and efficient and effective.

Confidence in e-government depends in a large part on the type of information floating around, through both electronic and nonelectronic formats and parts of the infrastructure, as well as the demographic using this information, and the purpose of the information. As seen in this study, trust in e-government has important impacts on the confidence in e-health, whereas increasing trust in e-government has no affect on concern for quality of health information. This may be because certain chronic care populations rely more heavily on charitable organizations for their health information, and those who rely most on this tend to care less about quality. Security of health information seems to be the most directly impacted by e-government, so this seems to be an important focus area, as those with the most trust in e-government will expect secure health information.

For these reasons, e-health legislation and initiatives led by e-governments are a difficult, yet important, endeavor. The practice of producing a beneficial e-government platform could be the solution to many barriers faced by citizens in interacting and using government resources. It also may have important implications in time, money, and interest for various stakeholders: citizens, residents, and the government.

The next chapter discusses the government's use of various policies to provide incentives for healthcare organizations, providers, hospitals, and smaller practices to utilize health information technologies. Chapter 3 analyzes the financial, sociocultural, and environmental purpose of various government initiatives, policies, and actions in deriving healthcare benefits.

# References

Center for Technology in Government. 2012. *A working definition of e-government.* Albany, NY: University of Albany.

Centers for Disease Control and Prevention. n.d. *Bridging the health literacy gap –Why usability matters to health literacy.* Online at: http://blogs.cdc.gov/healthliteracy/2012/07/17/why-usability-matters-to-health-literacy/ (accessed July 13, 2013).

Feldman, M. (2003). Building the Virtual State: Information Technology and Institutional Change, by Jane Fountain. Washington, DC: Brookings Institution Press, 2001, 256 pp., $13.95 paper. *Journal of Policy Analysis and Management*, 22(2), 324–326. doi:10.1002/pam.10127

Fountain, J. 2001. Building the virtual state: Information technology and institutional change. Washington, D.C.: Brookings Institution Press, p. 256; also see Feldman, M. 2003. *Journal of Policy Analysis and Management* 22 (2): 324–326.

Kennedy, E. M. 2005. The role of the federal government in eliminating health disparities. *Health Affairs* 24 (2): 452–458.

Koontz, L. D. 2004. *Electronic government: Initiatives sponsored by the Office of Management and Budget have made mixed progress.* Statement of Linda D. Koontz, director of Information Management Issues, before the subcommittee on Technology, Information Policy, Intergovernmental Relations and the Census, Committee on Government Reform, House of Representatives. Office of USGA, and Reform, USCHC on G.

Kules, B., and B. Xie. 2011. Older adults searching for health information in MedlinePlus—An exploratory study of faceted online search interfaces. Paper presented at the *Proceedings of the American Society for Information Science and Technology* 48 (1): 1–10.

Norman, C. D., and H. A. Skinner. 2006. eHEALS: The e-health literacy scale. *Journal of Medical Internet Research* 8 (4): e27.

*Office of E-Government & Information Technology.* n.d. Washington, D.C.: The White House, Office of Management and Budget. Online at: http://www.whitehouse.gov/omb/e-gov/docs (accessed July 13, 2013).

Rannu, R., Saksing, S., and Mahlakoiv, T. (2010). *Mobile Government: 2010 and Beyond White paper (eGovernment Resource Centre)* (Report). European Union Regional Development Fund. Retrieved from HYPERLINK "http://www.egov.vic.gov.au/trends-and-issues/mobile-government/mobile-government-2010-and-beyond-white-paper.html"http://www.egov.vic.gov.au/trends-and-issues/mobile-government/mobile-government-2010-and-beyond-white-paper.html

West, D. M., and E. A. Miller. 2006. The digital divide in public e-health: Barriers to accessibility and privacy in state health department websites. *Journal of Health Care for the Poor and Underserved* 17, 652–666.

World Bank, 2012. *Definition of e-government.* Washington, D.C.

## Chapter 3

# Financial, Social, and Environmental Impact of Government HIT Adoption Policies

## *Chapter Summary*

The objective of this chapter is to depict the slow rate of technology adoption across the U.S. healthcare industry, and provide potential reasons why there are differences in the rate of adoption across the industry. Provided is an analysis of the organizations that are having the most difficulty with electronic medical record (EMR) adoption and why purely financial (incentive payment) policies by the government are not affecting them. The Diffusion of Innovation Theory and the Social Contagion Theory are utilized to produce economic, social, and environmental barriers to EMR adoption (Rogers, 2003; Christakis and Fowler, 2013). These are primarily the economic policies of incentive payment systems that the United States has focused on in improving

EMR adoption rates. Because the current incentive payment policies (through "meaningful use" legislation) are unable to impact all healthcare providers, the author then discusses noneconomic policies of a sociocultural and environmental nature that are being implemented for small organizations that are slow to adopt health technology. The author discussed strengths and weaknesses to the social and environmental policies that have been introduced. Through a number of different types of policies, the government should be able to target all organizations and improve adoption rates across the industry, rather than favoring only some organizations that benefit from the current economic incentive payment structure. The chapter concludes with remarks on how the barriers and struggles are a part of the process that will provide a stronger set of solutions for those who have not adopted the technology, and why it has been a slow-moving process thus far.

## Assessment of the Barriers to Health Information Technology (HIT) Adoption across Organizations and the U.S. Policy Solutions

Health information technology (HIT) is a broad term that encompasses various types of health informatics tools, including the use of (1) electronic medical records (EMRs) or electronic health records (EHRs) in health provider settings, (2) personal health records (PHRs) primarily used by consumers, (3) telemedicine across organizations and geographic settings, as well as other types of electronic/mobile health devices. For this chapter, the author focuses on EMRs and EHRs for answering this question, just to provide clarity in answering why the EMR adoption rate varies across the health industry. Later chapters (such as Chapters 8 and 9) will provide greater clarity on the second and third objectives. The term *EMR* is used when referring to an intraorganization health information system, and *EHR* when referring to the interorganization health system. A recent Robert Wood Johnson Foundation (RWJF, 2013) reports trends in EHR adoption between 2006 and 2013 in the rate of technology adoption across the U.S. healthcare industry. For example, they suggest that about 80% of large, capital-rich organizations have adopted (certified or uncertified) EHRs, compared to about 40% of small, capital-poor organizations. Differences in EHR adoption persist across geographic areas, urban or rural settings, and the ownership status of the organization or practice (RWJF, 2013). Looking at this data, it is important to analyze the rate of adoption within the U.S. health industry to see what causes the differences in health information technology adoption, including economic, social, and environmental factors that may be slowing the rate of adoption for specific health providers.

There are many possible reasons for a slow rate of technology adoption, though the chapter focuses on three major reasons: economic, social, and environmental barriers to technology adoption. Theories that best represent the economic, social, and environmental barriers for adoption are discussed, followed by a description of each of the adoption barriers. The author then analyzes how the United States has tried to improve technology adoption through primarily economic policy changes, using an incentive payment system. There have been some challenges faced in using incentive payments as the primary policy to target technology adoption, because many organizations that do not qualify for the incentive payments are left out of this policy strategy.

Provided is an analysis of the organizations that are having the most difficulty with EMR adoption and why incentive payment policies are not affecting them. The majority of organizations that do not qualify are small practices that do not have a Medicare or Medicaid patient mix, or that do not adopt or correctly implement EMRs, which are supposed to be certified and follow "meaningful use" objectives. This is discussed more in detail in the following sections (Centers for Medicare and Medicaid Services, 2013). Because the current incentive payment policies (through "meaningful use" policies) are unable to impact all healthcare providers, the author introduces policy recommendations from a sociocultural and environmental angle that can be implemented for small organizations that are slow to adopt health technology. This way, the government should be able to target different types of organizations and improve adoption rates across the industry, rather than favoring only some organizations that benefit from a primarily economic, incentive payment structure. The author concludes with remarks on how the barriers and struggles are a part of the process that will provide a stronger set of solutions for those who have not adopted the technology, and it has been a slow-moving process thus far. The next section introduces the subject of technology adoption and provides a brief discussion on how different organizations are impacted by HIT.

## Organizational Variation in EMR Adoption

Health information technology adoption became a focus of the Health Information Technology for Economic and Clinical Health (HITECH) Act, a provision of the American Recovery and Reinvestment Act (ARRA) of 2009. The emphasis on an electronic health industry was primarily to produce savings in time and cost, while focusing on improved health outcomes, as noted by the Centers for Medicare and Medicaid Services (CMS). The HITECH Act is defined by the Office of the National Coordinator for Health Information Technology as legislation that furthers the organization of health information electronically to increase coordination and communication of health information, while reducing costs (ONC, 2012). In order to meet the objective of improving electronic exchanges of health information, the electronic medical/health record (EMR/EHR) became a vital component in the process of data exchange and delivery within and between healthcare providers. Many theorists have claimed that the EMR poses benefits as well as challenges in creating a wave of technology adoption across the United States. The author briefly discusses some of the advantages of EMR adoption, and then focuses on the economic, social, and environmental challenges in the section that follows.

The major benefits of the EMR affect multiple stakeholder groups: the patient, the physician, organizations, businesses, and the government, to name a few. Benefits to organizations are a major focus because this is the heart of much of the mainstream discussion on the issue. Healthcare organizations have estimated benefits from EMRs, which include (1) the EMR's ability to improve workflow and organizational speed/delivery of information, (2) the usage of the EMR to reduce redundancies and errors in health information documentation, and (3) increases in clinical objectives and guidelines, which can produce efficiencies and effectiveness in quality of care delivered (Restuccia et al., 2012; Jamoom et al., 2012; Simon, Rundall, and Shortell, 2007).

Research also suggests that there has been a lag in realizing these gains from technology adoption, especially across providers and health settings. The RWJF Report (2013) suggests that there is a disparity in technology adoption and realized gains from technology adoption across two major categories of organizations: (1) large, urban, and teaching hospitals, compared to (2) smaller, capital-poor, and rural hospitals and clinics. Nonprofit hospitals and for-profit hospitals have had great success with EMR adoption, and there are contradictory results on whether nonprofit hospitals are more successful than for-profit hospitals (Shih et al., 2012; Taylor et al., 2005). In general, hospitals have more capital to succeed at EMR adoption than smaller practices, which is why the author groups all hospitals except the federally sponsored hospitals, in the capital-rich, likely-to-adopt category. The discussion focuses on the differences in the adoption rates and challenges posed to these capital-rich hospitals that have an easier time adopting EMRs, compared to capital-poor, small practices and federal health centers that are lagging behind. The EMR adoption barriers faced are primarily of an economic, social, and environmental nature, and barriers affect the smaller organizations more so than the larger organizations. The chapter focuses on economic, social, and environmental barriers in explaining why technology adoption has not been equally distributed across capital-rich and capital-poor organizations.

Another category of organizations that are affected by EMR adoption and incentive programs by the government are government health centers, including federally qualified health centers (FQHCs) and community health centers (CHCs). Miller and West (2007) conducted a qualitative analysis on six community health centers (including FQHCs) in order to analyze the impact of EMRs on federal health centers between 2004 and 2005. They found that certain strengths were helping the CHCs with adoption, such as quality improvement (QI) strategies, but the amount of external financial support was not enough to sustain CHCs for long periods of time. To produce efficient use of resources, time, and money in EMR adoption across CHCs, government regulation has supported the access of FQHCs to regional extension centers (RECs) in order to facilitate EMR adoption (as well as RECs that provide support to small practices). This policy support strategy for small and government health centers will be discussed in greater detail in the social and environmental barriers section. It is included in the discussion of government clinics in the category of capital-poor organizations because most of the government hospitals depend on government grants and funding for their EMR usage and implementation.

The Diffusion of Innovation theory by Rogers (2003) provides a theoretical foundation for why there is a lag in the EMR adoption across the capital-rich (typically larger, reputed organizations) and capital-poor (typically smaller clinics and government funded) organizations and in the industry today, especially in understanding the economic and social barriers to adoption. Rogers depicts a curve where early adopters and innovators will have a higher perceived market share when working with a new innovation. The early adopters tend to be of greater financial status, primarily the capital-rich hospitals that can invest in expensive technologies and resources for implementation. On the other hand, Rogers' curve depicts that late adopters and laggards may face lower perceived market share and improvements from the technology adoption. Rogers' theory provides reasoning for why there is great disparity economically and socially across small and large health providers.

The Social Contagion theory is useful as well in understanding the social and environmental issues with technology adoption because the environment within technology diffusion may impact the likelihood and rate of EMR diffusion. An environment with many large hospitals may lead to even the smaller clinics in the area adopting new technologies, while an environment of capital-poor, unknown clinics may not be as interested or feel accountable for technology adoption. These theories point to the serious economic, sociocultural, and environmental differences in technology adoption because of the varied perception of technology usage and returns from technology adoption across organizations. The Diffusion of Innovation and Social Contagion theories will be used to discuss each barrier to technology adoption, and how government policies impact these barriers for specific types of organizations. The first barrier discussed is the economic barriers to technology adoption and how government policies, such as incentive payment structures, impact this barrier.

## Barriers to EMR Adoption

The author has documented three major reasons for the slow rate of EMR adoption across various health provider settings. These reasons include the economic barriers to EMR adoption, the social barriers to EMR adoption, and the environmental barriers to EMR adoption. The three factors produce specific differences in EMR adoption between capital-rich and capital-poor organizations. The capital-rich organizations, including large for-profit and nonprofit organizations have less difficulty with the economic costs of EMR adoption, and can overcome the social costs including the usability constraints, the stigma associated with new technologies, and the ethical problems that may arise in using EMRs. Capital-rich organizations may have the reputation and political incentives as well to adopt EMRs in comparison to the capital-poor organizations. The following documents each of the barriers to EMR adoption, beginning with the economic costs. It also documents the government policies in place that are trying to alleviate the economic barriers to EMR adoption, which are not successful for some of the capital-poor organizations.

## *Economic Costs of EMR Adoption*

The economic barriers to technology adoption are defined as the financial and usability costs of adopting and implementing HIT (Boonstra and Broekhuis, 2010). There are a number of different financial and technical costs to technology adoption, including upfront costs of implementation, ongoing costs of implementation and EMR usage, and financial difficulties faced during the system transition, as reported in a Behavioral Health Survey by the Office of National Coordinator (ONC) for HIT 2012 (National Council for Community Behavioral Healthcare, 2012). A large, capital-intense hospital may face some problems with the ability to adopt an EMR initially, but these sunk costs (costs already incurred) may be recuperated by meeting quality of care indicators, performance improvements, and government meaningful use policies (discussed next). On the other hand, smaller practices may not have the capital to invest in the sunk costs of an EMR system. These practices may have few personnel, limited salaries, and limited hours for learning new technologies, which are all resource constraints that impact EMR adoption.

The theory of Diffusion of Innovation is particularly useful in analyzing why there are such differences in the ability to adopt EMRs across providers (Rogers, 2003). In a study by Yan, Gardner, and Baier (2012), only 46% of physicians with EMRs faced renewed start-up financial costs, compared to nearly 80% of physicians without EMRs. Because the smaller practices are typically those that are late adopters in Rogers' Diffusion of Innovation model, the smaller practices may face higher renewed start-up costs, and the need for more upgrades than those who are early adopters and have had knowledge about the EMR from the beginning. Boonstra and Broekhuis (2010) found that a number of different financial costs posed barriers to EMR adoption, including start-up costs of capital, ongoing costs, and unknown return on investment (ROI) after implementation. The unknown perceived benefit of using the EMR is a particular problem discussed below in the section Social Barriers to Technology Adoption.

These financial difficulties are being ameliorated by the government's Meaningful Use policy (discussed in greater detail in the next section), but many small organizations are not incentivized to adopt EMRs, even in conjunction with the government Meaningful Use policies. There is a two-fold reason that small practices are not following Meaningful Use policies. One reason why many small practices aren't affected is because they do not accept Medicare or Medicaid, and, thus, they do not meet the requirements for Meaningful Use payments. The other reason is that many small practices face social and environmental barriers to EMR adoption (discussed below in Social Barriers to Technology Adoption and Environmental Barriers to Technology Adoption), which are not reflected in Meaningful Use incentive policies. The author provides examples of other government policies (the presence of RECs and Accountable Care Organizations (ACOs)) that are being used to impact the social and environmental structure of

EMR adoption for small practices, and also problems faced in implementing these policies. Before exploring the social and environmental challenges to EMR adoption, the author analyzes Meaningful Use and financial strategies to adopt EMRs in greater detail.

## Economic Policy Strategies to Help Organizations with Slow Rates of Adoption

Economic policies to improve EMR adoption have been the main focus of the government in improving these rates and implementation. The use of incentive payment plans has been a major part of the government overhaul in the move toward HIT, dictated by Meaningful Use policies of HIT. Meaningful Use policies require organizations with Medicare or Medicaid patient quotas to be properly implementing the EMR systems according to objectives from the CMS, and, in return, these organizations receive payments toward the cost of the EMR systems (Centers for Medicare and Medicaid Services, 2013). Meaningful Use Policies provide a maximum of $65,000 over 5 years per "eligible professional," or "EP," (professionals with at least 30 percent Medicaid patients) (if the physician began the EMR adoption process in 2011, less benefit if use EMR in 2013 or 2014, and no benefit if start adoption after 2015). Similarly, Meaningful Use Policies provide a maximum of about $44,000 over 5 years per eligible "Medicare oriented" professional (professionals with at least 30 percent Medicare patients) (if the physician began the EMR adoption process in 2011, less benefit if use EMR in 2013 or 2014, and no benefit if start adoption after 2015). There are penalties for physicians with Medicare and Medicaid who do not adopt an EHR system, beginning with 1 percent penalty of the Medicare physician fee schedule covered amount in 2015, 2 percent in 2016, and 3 percent in 2017 and the following years (Centers for Medicare and Medicaid, 2013).

There has been mixed results in the impact of these incentives on organizations. Poon et al. (2006) found that there were disparities in meaningful use of EMRs across hospitals, especially small, public, and rural hospitals as compared to large, private, and urban hospitals. There also seems to be difficulty in meeting the standards set by Meaningful Use. Poon et al. found that only 2% of the hospitals surveyed were meeting Meaningful Use criteria. To provide further reasons why many of these organizations are unable to meet meaningful use objectives, the author analyzed two other types of barriers to EMR usage and implementation: the social and environmental barriers. The social barriers include technical, ethical, and cultural reasons why organizations have difficulty adopting and, in turn, are unable to be incentivized by Meaningful Use policies, as well as environmental barriers that pose challenges based on social disparities and political consequences.

The financial barriers to EMR adoption have produced serious disparities in the adoption of EMRs across capital-rich and capital-poor organizations. Because the government incentive payments and economic policies alone are not useful in deriving change in HIT, especially for smaller organizations that do not qualify, the author looked to other reasons why organizations are unable to adopt EMRs and are not incentivized by the mainstream Meaningful Use policies. The government should focus on other types of policies targeting the social and environmental barriers to health technology adoption (discussed next), which will produce a more cohesive set of policy implications and adoption strategies.

## *Social Barriers to Technology Adoption*

Social factors that prevent technology adoption include (1) technical and usability issues with new technologies, (2) ignorance about perceived benefits as well as cultural stigma to electronics in healthcare, and (3) fear of privacy breaches, ethical issues, and government regulation that could occur with technology adoption, as the Diffusion of Innovation model and Social Contagion theory suggest. For example, the lack of data and research on the results from EMR adoption on quality of care and reduced costs leads to many smaller organizations that shy away from the technologies. The smaller organizations tend to be late adopters of the EMR, and may acquire little benefit in returns from adoption because of their delayed adoption. These organizations also have smaller networks with less social capital, which is why many of the smaller organizations don't find the presence of an EMR useful if they do not share data across an industry or region (Angst et al., 2010). Small organizations also find themselves fearing government regulation and presence in their businesses, and the presence of a certified EMR may only increase the risk that government can use or access small organizations' data.

The usability issues with technology adoption include the lack of technical skills and technical knowledge required to make the transition from paper to electronic reporting systems (Boonstra and Broekhuis, 2010). Synergy Health Solutions suggests that the technical difficulties faced by providers include the inability to customize the EMR to the physicians' workflow, and the inability to train staff to support the EMRs and EMR rollout process (Synergy Health Solutions, 2010). This issue is exacerbated for smaller organizations that don't have the capital to invest in training, staff, resources, and the time to learn the new technology. Larger hospitals may have fewer problems with the usability and technical troubles due to the financial ability to invest in the transition to new technologies. Kadry et al. (2010) found that the integration of large amounts of data across clinical information systems was a difficult, time consuming, and expensive process, regardless of vendor, because of the complex nature of the database architecture. This is another issue that affects many organizations and would particularly affect smaller practices that don't have economic, social, and environmental support in making the transition.

Coupled with usability issues, Boonstra and Broekhuis (2010) found that 92% of physicians felt that EMRs were a disturbance between the patient and the physician and may introduce issues of longer wait times in the appointment when the EMR did not function correctly. For small practices that are primarily focused on a market of word-of-mouth customers, there is fear that a new system may shake the consistency and reputation built within the clinic (Casalino et al., 2009). Ethical and privacy policies also become an issue for EMR adoption across small and large practices. At the same time, with new Health Information Portability and Accountability Act (HIPAA) standards in place, there can be advantages and disadvantages to trusting that HIPAA will help organizations provide secure health information storage (Casalino et al., 2009). The advantages to HIPAA include an easier flow of information with encryption, and the disadvantages may be the presence of privacy breaches through EMRs. The social stigma toward systems that may be hacked or have security threats are a possible reason for lack of adoption. Another potential perception of HIPAA is that it promotes the presence of government in the usage of the EMR and data transfer, which is particularly negatively perceived by small practices (Casalino et al., 2009). Again, smaller practices less likely to be in favor of a system where regulation and government guidelines restrict their independence.

## Social Policies to Help Organizations That Are Unable to Adopt EMRs

As discussed under the economic policy solutions, incentive payments may not be useful in targeting many of the socio-cultural stigmas and barriers to EMR adoption, especially for smaller practices. Rather, an important government policy that has already been instated to impact social consequences to technology adoption has been the presence of the RECs, which are organizations that provide information and training support to smaller organizations that adopt health technologies. RECs were created by the HITECH Act, and may vary across states based on funding and policy initiatives toward HIT delivery and technology usage. RECs are stand-alone centers that may provide training, education, and resources (webinars, seminars) on the best uses of EMRs as well as the transition from paper-based records to electronic records (Office of the National Coordinator for HIT, 2012).

Through the presence of RECs at small practices, the adoption of EMRs and EHRs was about 8 percentage points higher, or 79% for providers working with RECs, compared to providers working without REC help. On the other hand, some studies suggest that RECs have not had perceived benefits. For example, Ryan et al. (2013) suggest that technical assistance, such as support of RECs, is needed in EMR implementation for many small practices. Ryan et al. analyzed a project in New York City, known as the Primary Care Information Project, to gauge the impact of technical assistance from RECs on small practices in underserved neighborhoods. The effect of RECs was minimal and only significant after a period of nine months of extensive levels of help for small practices. Similarly, in the Mississippi Regional Extension Centers, nearly 800 practices that were using the RECs already had an EMR, compared to only 300 that did not have an EMR and had enrolled with a REC for help (AMedNews, 2012). Government health centers also have received support from RECs, though research does not suggest specific benefits that have been realized thus far. An ONC Data Brief in 2013 suggests that nearly 83% of FQHCs and FQHC look-alikes were receiving help from the RECs, so RECs have served as useful sources of economic support to the FQHCs. Not enough research focuses on the exact services that RECs deliver, and the types of care they deliver at health organizations, from a sociocultural perspective.

Other government policies that are not primarily financial in nature may be very useful. For example, having webinars with reduced fees for smaller organizations to understand the consequences of the EMR usage, and portals and forums for exchanging knowledge and experience on EMR usage may be useful for smaller practices that are weary of technology adoption. Examples of Web portals that are designed for this purpose include Physicians Practice and EMR News (electronic news), which documents new trends, impacts, and changes in the industry.

Some of the social barriers to EMR adoption include the complexity of EMR systems, social stigma to using EMRs due to unknown return on investment, and fear of privacy threats—HIPAA violations that can impact the practices' reputation. In order to provide policy support for the social barriers to EMR adoption, the government currently has implemented RECs in disadvantaged neighborhoods and rural areas. Other policies that may provide support include the presence of webinars and Web forums to help organizations make the transition through peer support groups that will tackle the many technical, usability, and fear-driven reasons for lack of EMR adoption. Next, the author analyzes the environmental issues that may be stopping EMR adoption.

## Environmental Barriers to Technology Adoption

The environmental barriers to technology adoption may be due to differences in social capital and political power in the health industry. These environmental effects produce disparities between organizations rich in resources and reputation, compared to those with lower social capital and political power in the health industry. The presence of larger organizations that have received Stage 7 Meaningful Use status suggests that larger organizations may be more likely to achieve EMR adoption and full EMR implementation because of economic and reputational incentives that drive better results. The environmental impacts of EMR adoption may be founded on the Social Contagion theory.

The Social Contagion theory by Christakis and Fowler (2012) and Monge and Contractor (2003) suggests that larger organizations may be more likely to adopt health technologies than smaller organizations because of differences in social capital, and differences in a social reputation that drives their incentive to thrive in the markets. For example, larger for-profit and non-profit organizations (such as Hospital Corporation of American and Kaiser Permanente) that are competing for the HIMSS (Health Information Management Systems Society) Davies Stage 7 award may be more likely to adopt EMRs to produce a higher status and gain more market share, reputation, and patients than organizations that are not competing for market share and are not resource intense. For example, Ludwick, Manca, and Doucette (2010) found that there was a lower EMR adoption rate for physicians of community and suburban hospitals, as compared to physicians in "urban, hospital, and academic settings" in Alberta, Canada. Through a qualitative analysis, semistructured interviews helped discover features of the urban hospital setting that were not found to be present in the rural community. For example, many physicians in urban settings could "leverage professional working relationships to investigate EMRs," which was helpful in EMR adoption. These social networks and relationships can particularly impact the presence of innovation in an organization. Another set of studies found that organizational climate was not strictly dependent on nonprofit or for-profit status, but on how resource rich that organization was and the environment of the organization. Many nonprofits that are in settings near profit organizations and compete with for-profit organizations may actually have higher EMR adoption rates, even though they are not incentivized by a profit margin (Taylor et al., 2005). On the other hand, differences persist across small providers and large providers, especially resource-abundant, politically empowered providers and resource-poor, small providers (RWJF, 2012). The description of the ACOs, discussed next, depicts how politics plays a role in producing environmental barriers to EMR adoption.

## Environmental Policy Strategies to Help Organizations with Slow Rates of Adoption

The environmental barriers to technology adoption are not aided by the government's incentive payment policies. The government has made only one indirect policy effort to impact the social contagion effect of EMR adoption: the creation of accountable care organizations (ACOs). The ACOs function to improve data exchange, especially for organizations with Medicare and Medicaid, through increased interaction and data sharing between organizations within certain areas. The ACOs are linked to a health information exchange because they utilize technologies to collect and coordinate data across the EHRs at various ACO members' locations. Yet, this only produces a greater disparity for those organizations, especially smaller organizations that don't have a Medicare or Medicaid patient mix. The majority of ACOs currently include larger, capital-rich hospitals, providers, and physicians' offices (Healthcare Finance News, 2013).

The American Medical Association (AMA) has been particularly against the presence and proposed guidelines of ACOs (Healthcare Finance News, 2013). The AMA claims that the ACOs are hurting small practices by keeping out practices with less than 10 employees, a violation of antitrust laws. The AMA reported on the projected difficulties in small practices being a part of the ACOs because of limited resources, and how this could lower the projected value of the ACOs' original objective, which is risk sharing and accountability of all providers in the community. The violation that AMA suggests is due to the likelihood that most ACOs will consist of HMOs, insurance companies, and large hospitals, with the resources on the health information exchange to conduct business. Rather than creating new competition, this could worsen the already problematic state that small practices are currently in (Healthcare Finance News, 2013). Research is still lacking on exactly how many small practices are going to be affected, and possibly derailed by the presence of ACOs. Communities with ACOs may see fewer private practices in their locality, unless policy solutions are provided to enhance the state of small practices so that they can compete with, or be a part of, the ACO model.

For this reason, the ACO model has not been particularly useful as a policy strategy for alleviating environmental barriers to EMR adoption. Rather, there is need for organizations that mediate ACOs and makes them more usable and accessible to smaller practices, which may produce a desirable effect and increase and promote EMR adoption and implementation across these smaller practices.

The environmental barriers to EMR adoption are dependent on the economic status and social capital of an organization, which also may provide the organization with greater financial and political support in adopting EMRs. Typically, large hospitals are driven by market incentives, reputation, and competition against other providers to improve their EMR adoption and implementation rates. Smaller and capital-poor organizations are unable to develop the social networks and political support for interacting in health information transfers. This problem has been heightened by the presence of ACOs, which has led to fragmented groups of power in the struggle for EMR adoption in the community. The last section provides final thoughts on the state of EMR adoption across health providers in the United States, major barriers posed to providers across health settings, and the advantages and disadvantages of government policies that are meant to alleviate the barriers present.

## Conclusion

There is still a lag in the presence of EMRs across organizations in the United States, particularly differences between capital-rich and capital-poor organizations. Yet, economic factors are not the only major contributor to the lag in EMR adoption. If this was the case, the presence of government incentive payments, from Meaningful Use provisions, would be enough to counter the economic barriers to EMR adoption. Rather, there are serious social and environmental barriers to EMR adoption, including problems with technical feasibility, privacy concerns, interest and perceived benefits, as well as reputation, and political concerns with EMR adoption. In order to counter some of the social and environmental problems with EMR adoption, the author analyzed a few of the government policies, such as the creation of RECs and ACOs that were meant to bolster the EMR adoption rate in rural, disadvantaged, and politically weak organizations. The REC and ACO government policies are still facing challenges, much like the Meaningful Use provisions, in targeting small-practice providers to increase EMR adoption, because they are unable to unearth the social capital struggles between capital-rich and capital-poor organizations. For this reason, there is still need for increased information, participation, and government marketing of health information technologies as well as research on the benefits of EMRs and how they can improve the state of healthcare delivery for all kinds of health organizations, including smaller practices. This way, the use of government incentive payment policies, RECs, and ACOs will be more beneficial in reducing the disparities across EMR adoption and produce an improvised, utilitarian HIT industry.

Part I discussed a general introduction to healthcare reform and health information technology. Part II provided health information technology solutions that were provided by the government. Next, Part III will discuss individual-level solutions to chronic conditions and health problems when coupled with HIT.

# References

AMedNews. 2012. Will concierge medicine's image improve as it evolves? March 9. Online at: http://www.amednews.com/article/20120903/profession/309039953/5/ (accessed May 9, 2013).

Angst, C. M., R. Agarwal, V. Sambamurthy, and K. Kelley. 2010. Social contagion and information technology diffusion: The adoption of electronic medical records in U.S. hospitals. *Management Science* 56 (8): 1219–1241.

Boonstra, A., and M. Broekhuis. 2010. Barriers to the acceptance of electronic medical records by physicians from systematic review to taxonomy and interventions. *BMC Health Services Research* 10 (1): 231.

Casalino, L. P., D. Dunham, M. H. Chin, R. Bielang, E. O. Kistner, T. G. Karrison, and D. O. Meltzer. 2009. Frequency of failure to inform patients of clinically significant outpatient test results. *Archives of Internal Medicine* 169 (12): 1123–1129.

Centers for Medicare and Medicaid Services. 2013. Meaningful Use. Online at: http://www.cms.gov/Regulations-and-Guidance/Legislation/EHRIncentivePrograms/Meaningful_Use.html (accessed May 23, 2013).

Christakis, N. A., and J. H. Fowler. 2013. Social contagion theory: Examining dynamic social networks and human behavior. *Statistics in Medicine* 32 (4): 556–577.

Healthcare Finance News. n.d. AMA asks for ACO changes in support of small practices. Online at: http://www.healthcare-financenews.com/news/ama-asks-aco-changes-support-small-practices (accessed May 9, 2013).

Jamoom et al. 2012. *Physician adoption of electronic health record systems: United States, 2011.* NCHS data brief No. 98. Online at: http://medicalmastermind.acd.netdna-cdn.com/wp-content/uploads/2012/11/Physician-Adoption-of-Electronic-Health-Record-Systems-US-2011.pdf.

Kadry, B., W. W. Feaster, A. Macario, and J. M. Ehrenfeld. 2012. Anesthesia Information Management Systems: Past, present, and future of anesthesia records. *Mount Sinai Journal of Medicine: A Journal of Translational and Personalized Medicine* 79 (1): 154–165.

Ludwick, D., D. Manca, and J. Doucette. 2010. Primary care physicians' experiences with electronic medical records: Implementation experience in community, urban, hospital, and academic family medicine. *Canadian Family Physician* 56 (1): 40–47.

Miller, R. H., and C. E. West. 2007. The value of electronic health records in community health centers: Policy implications. *Health Affairs* 26 (1): 206–214.

Monge, P., and N. Contractor. 2003. *Theories of communication networks.* New York: Oxford University Press.

ONC. (2012). Retrieved from http://www.healthit.gov/

Restuccia, J. D., A. B. Cohen, J. N. Horwitt, and M. Shwartz. 2012. Hospital implementation of health information technology and quality of care: Are they related? *BMC Medical Informatics and Decision Making* 12 (1): 10.

Robert Wood Johnson Foundation (RWJF). 2013. Measuring adoption and use of health information technology to reduce health care disparities and improve quality. Online at: http://www.rwjf.org/en/research-publications/find-rwjf-research/2012/08/measuring-adoption-and-use-of-health-information-technology-to-r.html (accessed May 5, 2013).

Rogers, E. M. 2003. *Diffusion of innovations.* New York: Free Press.

Ryan, A. M., T. F. Bishop, S. Shih, and L. P. Casalino. 2013. Small physician practices in New York needed sustained help to realize gains in quality from use of electronic health records. *Health Affairs* 32 (1): 53–62.

Shin, D. Y., Menachemi, N., Diana, M., Kazley, A. S., and Ford, E. W. (2012). Payer mix and EHR adoption in hospitals. *Journal of healthcare management/American College of Healthcare Executives,* 57(6), 435–448; discussion 449–450.

Simon, J. S., T. G. Rundall, and S. M. Shortell. 2007. Adoption of order entry with decision support for chronic care by physician organizations. *Journal of the American Medical Informatics Association* 14 (4): 432–439.

Taylor, R., A. Bower, F. Girosi, J. Bigelow, K. Fonkych, and R. Hillestad. 2005. Promoting health information technology: Is there a case for more-aggressive government action? *Health Affairs* 24 (5): 1234–1245.

Yan, H., R. Gardner, and R. Baier. 2012. Beyond the focus group: Understanding physicians' barriers to electronic medical records. *Joint Commission Journal on Quality and Patient Safety/Joint Commission Resources* 38 (4): 184–191.

# INDIVIDUALIZED TECHNOLOGICAL PREVENTION STRATEGIES FOR CHRONIC CONDITIONS

# Chapter 4

---

# Self-Management Technologies and Type 2 Diabetes

---

## *Chapter Summary*

This chapter researches the social, ethical, and financial impacts of self-management technologies (Web-based interventions, mobile health applications and resources, and video games) on patients with type 2 diabetes who are responsible for managing their own condition.

Diabetes has been a costly illness for the United States and many other nations, and is a leading cause of other chronic conditions, such as obesity, cardiovascular disease, and increasing mortality rates. Computer-based interventions have suggested improving outcomes for individuals to identify and manage chronic health conditions, cut costs, and improve quality of life. Inclusion criteria states that only patients who have type 2 (self-inflicted) diabetes and used self-management tools for controlling their diabetes were selected for the analysis.

Evidence-based information was found by searching systematic reviews and findings from various medical and health journals and the Cochrane database. Information on ethics, costs, and social constraints through the use of computer-based intervention tools on health outcomes were the primary target of searches. Some of the studies were cross-sectional in nature, whereas the randomized controls were typically over a short, six-month to one-year period. About 10 high-quality, evidence-based articles were analyzed (including RCTs (randomized controlled trials), meta-analysis, and systematic reviews), whereas another 10 were of the fair- or poor-quality evidence (reports, books from experts, qualitative studies, and news articles). A great deal of the literature focused on online Web-based applications, though fewer, newer articles and research discuss mobile health technologies and video games. Resources from all three categories were found to have at least one positive impact on health outcomes and health management, typically in behavioral outcomes (positive reinforcement, motivation, raising awareness, and knowledge on a subject, or making some difference to lifestyle changes). None of these had a negative impact on health, but some studies suggested no effect, especially to biological outcomes (blood pressure, BMI (base mass index), cholesterol levels, etc.). Implications of cost and ethics were not transparently stated in the studies and must be analyzed from a policymaking perspective. The various tools may be weighted for their benefits based on costs and their ethical constraints. Policy implications involved the short- and long-term advantages and disadvantages for granting more research and subsidies for self-management technology projects and usage, as well as ethical, financial, and social consequences of self-management technologies on individuals. Political issues and regulations in the market also impact the sale and utilization of self-management technologies.

# The Effects of Self-Management Technologies on Type 2 Diabetes Patients

## *Purpose*

The research question discusses the impacts of self-management devices (online Web portals and Web applications, mobile health devices, and video game health management devices) on health outcomes for diabetic patients. The hypothesis is that self-management devices will have no effect on the health status of diabetic patients. This hypothesis will be disproved if these devices impact the self-management of care in some manner, either through changes in health outcomes, reduced costs, by providing education, awareness, coordination, and/or monitoring. The study holds race, income, education, and other socioeconomic and demographic features constant. Patients using the technology must primarily manage their own diabetes, such that their clinician or caregiver is not their only source of care management.

## *Introduction and Background*

Much literature discusses the growing presence of technology usage by chronic disease patients to manage their own care. Examples of such technology include computer devices, mobile health (m-health) tools, and patient controlled health records (PHRs). There is evidence suggesting that technology usage in chronic care self-management has social, financial, and ethical implications on the patient and the community.

The benefits of self-management in chronic care for patients and the community are debated in the literature, which is why more policy research needs to be done on the subject. If the technology seems to be positively impacting the health outcome of patients who manage their chronic disease, there will be a demand for allocating time and money toward self-management technologies. To narrow the searches of past literature to specific forms of technology, only computer-based and mobile health technologies were analyzed in this chapter, with a focus on short-run consequences.

Self-management technologies are defined in this study as tools serving different social purposes, including educating, controlling a disease, controlling lifestyle conditions linked to the disease (nutrition, fitness, etc.), and providing updates on information regarding the disease through the tool's digital presence. There are three different types of devices discussed in this study: online Web-based interventions and Web applications, mobile health devices and related mobile phone applications, and video game health management devices. Personal health records were not a part of this study, because they primarily test storage of data and have data-driven outcomes versus the goal of improving health outcomes, which is the primary focus of this study.

Some examples of self-management technologies include Packy and Marlon™ (Super Nintendo Entertainment), a diabetes management video game, as well as online computer programs, such as Diabetes NetPLAY,™ and Google mobile applications, such as OnTrack Diabetes™ and Glucool Diabetes™ (Liebreich et al., 2009). Packy and Marlon is a video game targeted for kids under the age of 18, and has had positive results—nearly 77% fewer diabetes-related urgent care and emergency room visits over six months. The intervention group was compared to those not assigned to play the game. Other systems like OnTrack Diabetes provide virtual testing, allowing an individual to change and tailor parts of their lifestyle (diet, exercise, and insulin usage) to the diabetes, while recording impacts through software documentation. The software provides tips, ideas, and possibilities for enhancing and optimizing diabetes management, which may provide social benefits. Diabetes NetPLAY™ has had positive impacts on increased physical activity by patients. Some of the latest mobile health tools and applications, such as OnTrack Diabetes,™ do not have studies presenting their outcomes, so literature on these applications are from blogs or expert interviews rather than evidence-based systematic reviews.

State and federal government initiatives are providing financial incentives and funding for technology-based solutions for management of chronic disease. The Health Information Technology and Economic Health (HITECH) Act, a provision of the American Recovery and Reinvestment Act of 2009 (ARRA), has provided federal funding toward a technologically linked infrastructure for the United States in hopes of improving health outcomes. Medical device integration, the creation of an electronic medical record system and incorporation of patient-controlled health records, funding for research on self-management devices, and creation of the health information exchanges are virtual changes to the health system, which are driven by both federal and state efforts. Guidelines for security, privacy, and regulation provided by federal legislation also may impact the creation, supply, and demand of the various self-management technologies.

Yet, the health economics of the health technology (self-management technology) market impacts various community members differently. Primary care providers may view the use of electronic self-management tools as a possible help or a hindrance. They may be impacted by a lack of demand for their expertise due to the wealth of information available in online portals and mobile health information. At the same time, there may be efficiency and cost savings from providing their patients a digital portal for care. Private technology companies also may use the demand for self-management devices as an economic opportunity, with predatory pricing and possibly a market of untested and unnecessary products. Patients have the risk of exacerbating health problems if incorrectly treating their own condition with such products. This could later burden our healthcare system with even higher costs if there are technological mishaps or patient mismanagement of chronic conditions.

## Policy Relevance

Legislation has important repercussions on various stakeholders and society using this diabetes management technology. The HITECH Act prompted the use of self-management technologies through funding initiatives, research about self-management technologies, and grants to organizations with electronic health records, usage of patient controlled health records, and other technologies that may be interoperable with self-management technologies. On the other hand, the Patient Protection and Affordable Care Act (PPACA) led to changes in HIPAA (Health Insurance Portability and Accountability Act), which now has more safety and security regulations on patient medical records and confidential information. Many of the guidelines of the Genetic Information Nondiscrimination Act (GINA), similarly has importance for patients with chronic care and genetic diseases, as their privacy could be breached if their genetic information is misused by physicians, outside organizations, or corporations. How, and if, this applies to self-management technologies that are sold on the market is still to be explored. These various legislative pieces have demonstrated a reciprocal relationship between technology, laws, security, and privacy for consumers.

While patients may not need to interact with a provider when using self-management mobile health and computer programs, the use of linked electronic records to patient-controlled records and self-management technologies in the future may cause gray areas in management of care for the role of electronic prescribing, electronic lab results, and more.

## Theoretical Backing

There is one theory that supports the need for patient self-management programs using technology. This is the Chronic Care Model, or CCM, used by Norris, Engelgau, and Narayan (2001), described in Figure 4.1.

The Chronic Care Model was developed by two Washington State-based research organizations, Group Research Health Institute and the MacColl Institute for Healthcare Innovation, to strategize techniques for improving healthcare through technology usage. The major elements in the model are "the community, the health system, self-management support, delivery system design, and decision support and clinical information systems." Efficiency and effectiveness of technology integration in the CCM can be done by (1) developing tools for patients to take an active part in their care and (2) guiding markets on safer and better technology marketing to patients. The CCM can be applied to a variety of chronic illnesses, healthcare settings, and target populations to improve problems with meeting established

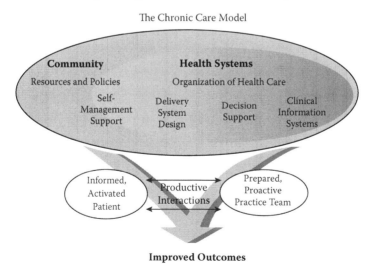

**Figure 4.1   The Chronic Care Model. (From The MacColl Institute ACP-ASEM journals and book. With permission.)**

practice guidelines, care coordination, inactive follow-ups, and inadequate self-management training for patients. Outcomes projected through the CCM are improvements in quality of care, with the presence of healthier patients and more satisfied providers as well as cost savings.

The social, financial, and ethical aspects of technology usage in patient self-management of chronic conditions overlap. Social and/or ethical impacts on patient technology usage may drive financial consequences. Financial impacts on patients may drive social and ethical consequences for the patient as well. All of these aspects need to be considered when analyzing whether patients are truly benefiting from the usage of technology in their chronic disease management. These will be discussed in the latter part of the analysis.

## Methods

Past literature provides examples of the impacts of computer-based interventions on diabetes management. Some literature consists of systematic reviews, which are culminations of published literature and their tests of self-management devices on health outcomes. Other literature includes studies of randomized control trials that test patients who use the computer interventions for their disease management, compared to groups that do not. Sources of the material are from the Cochrane Library database, *PubMed*, *Medline*, and other medical journals. Literature is grouped into three categories: Web-based/online technologies, computer and video game technologies, and mobile health technologies.

Keyword searches were used to identify material that best portrays the subject of interest. Examples of the keywords for the material included "mobile health interventions," "diabetes self-management," "Web interventions for diabetes self-management," "DSM (diabetes self-management)," and more specific names of technologies, such as "Glucoboy" and "OnTrackDiabetes App."

Literature was collected through a selective inclusion process. While a total of 50 studies were analyzed, only 8 papers met the selection criteria to be analyzed. The selection criteria included patients (1) diagnosed with type 2 diabetes, and (2) who were using a computer or mobile-based self-management tool, be it Web-based interactions, Ipads, mobile devices, or stand-alone monitors. Some evidence-based studies from the Cochrane Library were analyzed, but only two systematic reviews met the selection criteria. The majority of studies were randomized control trials.

Being a new subject of relevance to communities across the globe, the study accepted studies from all countries, which provided greater information, better comparisons, and an understanding of how findings may differ by geographic context. Age, gender, and ethnicity were not restrictions. The date of selection was within the past 10 years, from 2002 through 2012, though much of the literature was in the past five years.

Quality varied across studies, as Table 4.1 demonstrates. A total of three types of literature were considered high quality and evidence-based: one that was a meta-analysis, two that were systematic reviews, and seven studies that were RCTs. All of these high-quality studies received a ranking of 3. A total of three studies provided fair evidence, receiving a ranking of 2. They were either books written by experts in the field, or a qualitative study that did not involve a randomized research design. Finally, three studies were quite inconclusive, as they provided limited scientific advice, but were pertinent for their timeliness in news pieces, editorials, or self-management technology reviews. They provide insights on how diabetic patients felt about the technology without strong evidence to support their conclusions. These studies received a ranking of 1. No studies were pulled that completely lacked scientific evidence or expert opinions. These studies would have received a ranking of zero.

**Table 4.1    Categorization of the Medicine Literature Based on the Study Design**

| Number of Publications | Strength Level: 3 = Highest; 0 = Lowest | Supporting Rationale and Study Design | Ranking |
|---|---|---|---|
| 1 meta-analysis<br><br>2 systematic reviews of RCTs<br><br>7 RCTs | 3 | Systematic reviews consisting of:<br><br>1. Meta-analysis<br><br>2. Small (n) studies that include well-defined research questions | Strong evidence |
| 3 total<br><br>1 qualitative study<br><br>2 books by experts in the field | 2 | Fair evidence<br><br>Limited scientific information with potential for bias, such as systematic reviews, case reports, etc. | Fair evidence<br><br>Non-RCT, small (n) original research with statistical analysis and a potential for bias |
| 3 | 1 | Expert opinion and/or limited scientific information with potential for significant bias, such as editorials, commentaries, policy forum, etc. | Inconclusive Evidence |
| 0 | 0 | No scientific information | Evidence lacking |

## Results

The following is evidence of three types of self-management tools for diabetic patients: online Web-based applications and resources for managing care, mobile health technologies, and video game-based health tools. The differences in these tools is that some are free or low in cost, such as the Web-based technologies, whereas video games and mobile health technologies may be too expensive for the general public to afford. There also may be group differences within age groups using the above technologies and differences in perception of usefulness.

## *Web-Based Technologies*

Web-based technology applications showed the following outcomes. McKay et al. (2001) completed a study on physical activity intervention on 78 type 2 diabetic patients, who were randomly provided the Diabetes Network (D-Net) Active Lives PA Intervention. This program provided the following to its patients: "goal-setting and personalized feedback," identifying and developing "strategies to overcome barriers," receiving and posting messages to an "online personal coach," and providing "peer group support areas" (p. 1,328). It was found that those using the intervention a greater number of times derived benefit on two main outcomes measures: moderate to intensive physical activity and depressive symptoms. The number of logons to Internet Web pages and number of pages visited were higher with the intervention group. Statistical significance was found for changes in moderate to physical intensity, but no change in mood for depressive symptoms was seen.

In a similar study to the last, McKay et al. (2002) studied "The Diabetes Network (D-Net), a randomized trial of an Internet-based, diabetes self-management and peer support intervention," over a three-month period. It differs from the last study because they test health outcomes that were physiological *and* mental. Methods included multivariate general linear models to evaluate the effects of personalized self-management and of peer support and to adjust for baseline values. The study assessed impacts of the PSMCC (personalized self-management coach condition), intervention that include: (a) physiological outcomes (total cholesterol and HbA1c, dietary behavior (dietary practices such as fat screener), and mental health outcomes (CES-D and SF-12). There was one marginally significant multivariate effect favoring the personalized self-management conditions for mental health outcomes using Wilks's lambda at a .08 significance level. The encouraging effects of the intervention were on dietary behavior change, especially on the fat screener measure. It does not appear, however, that these changes impacted improvements of a biological nature or improvements in mental health in the short term during which the study was conducted. Yet, a positive finding is that presence of misinformation when using diabetes for Web searches and education was not observed in the study.

Kim and Kang (2006) used a Web-based program to detect impacts on three health measures: physical activity, fasting blood sugar, and glycosylated hemoglobin, through a randomized control process. T-tests were used for understanding statistical significance between printed and Web-based interventions as well as printed interventions, Web-based interventions, and normal care. While there is significance in Web-based interventions and printed materials compared to lack of these resources, there was no statistical significance between Web interventions and printed materials, as long as one of the two were provided.

Ramadas et al. (2011) explore a Web-based dietary intervention to analyze impacts on the dietary knowledge, attitudes, and behaviors (KAB) for diabetic patients in Malaysia. The study completed a randomized control trial of 82 type 2 diabetics with the Web-based technology intervention for a six-month period supplementing standard diabetes care versus those of the comparison group, just the standard diabetes care. The objective of the study was to measure change in the KAB score in participants of the e-intervention group, besides investigating the impact of the e-intervention on the dietary practices, physical measurements, and blood biomarkers of those patients. This trial is in intervention mode and will be completed within the next year. T-tests and chi-squared tests were completed to analyze differences between the intervention group and comparison group in their blood glucose control and complications from diabetes.

Leeman-Castillo et al. (2010) and Glasgow et al. (2010) discuss diabetes self-management (DSM) programs using comparisons of different technologies. Using a randomized control trial, the study analyzes how technology-based programs and routine care programs impact behavioral outcomes: healthy eating, fat intake, physical activity, and taking of medication. Biological outcomes, such as hemoglobin A1c, body mass index, lipids, and blood pressure, also were tested. Changes to healthy eating, fat intake, and physical activity were seen, but biological outcomes were not. This particular program, called LUCHAR, was used for Spanish-speaking Latinos. In the past, Latinos have been most impacted by the digital divide, which is why the study seemed to add a new insight to this body of research. LUCHAR improved nutrition and physical outcomes.

From these findings, there is evidence to suggest that many Web-based technologies (the majority that are free of cost) are providing supplemental help through data and information collection, a support to diabetic patients. Much of the other literature is debated as to whether there are physiological, behavioral, or mental health behavior differences from the use of such technologies. While financial constraints are minor, because most online tools are free or low cost, issues, such as the digital divide in using the Web, ethical issues of incorrect information, and personal bias, may still persist as suggested by Piette (2002).

## Mobile and Telephone Interventions

The use of both telephone (mobile and wired connections) interventions has been documented and is of relevance to the study of self-management tools for diabetes patients.

A study by Bird et al. (2010) analyzed a phone-based self-management intervention for Australian patients with type 2 diabetes over a six-month period through a randomized control trial. The participants received both a study handbook and a glucose meter linked to a data uploading device, which helps with monitoring and "tailored feedback and education on key aspects of diabetes self-management." Major outcomes studied were patient's quality of life and cost effectiveness of the treatment, compared to routine care alone. The cost effectiveness is measured as quality-adjusted life years (QALYs), which impacts the cost-utility ratio of the intervention. Probabilistic sensitivity analysis also was used to test the study rather than a traditional sensitivity analysis. Probabilistic sensitivity analysis provided the advantage of testing uncertainties in all values simultaneously (a method founded by Doubilet et al., 1985).

Arsand et al. (2010) discuss Few Touch Application, an application that is a multipurpose, integrated portal for diabetes management to promote a healthy diet, blood glucose (BG) management, and physical activity. This qualitative study looked at a variety of perspectives on patient interaction with self-management technologies. Few Touch Application is a mobile phone application studied to analyze whether such systems could motivate and support type 2 diabetes patients, while improving their overall health outcomes and interest. The system worked well in motivating individuals, but problems, such as boredom to report and misreporting due to personal bias, were present. Overall such interventions were not presenting an increased burden on patients.

Methods for the test included qualitative techniques: a questionnaire, focus groups, paper prototyping, prototyping of both software and hardware components, and basic demographic data to analyze the likelihood of increasing various diet, exercise, and goal setting. A positive improvement was seen in blood glucose levels for patients from Few Touch. Indirect impacts on health outcomes were seen on patients who were eating a healthier diet (more fruits and vegetables), as they increased their number of steps walked. They also found that mobile health texts provided tips on a healthier diet, and provided a good monitor of their progress.

Other studies discuss cost effectiveness of self-monitoring technologies (as opposed to self-management), like Cameron et al. (2010). Their study suggests that type 2 diabetes patients (who don't use insulin) did not see any improvements through the use of blood glucose test strips for self-monitoring, nor was it cheaper or more efficient to use self-monitoring devices. Periodic testing seemed to be more cost-effective than everyday usage. Another conclusion was that reduced test strip prices may contribute to cost-effectiveness. Self-management programs also may be significantly impacted by their duration, indicated by Norris et al. (2001).

## Video Games

Gee (2007) theorizes that games are an effective tool for learning, especially in learning associated with health behaviors. While monitoring of diabetes using video games has primarily been for a younger age group, this is still an option for those who are younger or college aged with type 2 (not type 1 or juvenile) diabetes. There were only a few findings regarding this subject that applied to type 2 diabetes patients. There were positive results that suggest that short-term goals set by the video games assisted in short- and long-term improvements in health goals and outcomes.

Findings suggest that this tool can promote awareness, education, interaction, and communication among children and their providers or parents about health information. Examples besides the earlier mentioned Packy and Marlon video game includes Bronkie the Brachiosaurus, Prisoner's Dilemma, and more (Brown, 1998). Habit creation was another outcome of these video games. The way in which the correlation between improved scores in the game and improved health outcomes was achieved is by providing points through health education and learning. As players "score" through improvements in their health management goals, they are able to increase their score. Typically, as a two-player game, these games can increase communication between players about the outcomes and health.

Another product suggested by Brown (1998) is Glucoboy, an Australian blood glucose meter (used to test blood), which combines an element of positive reinforcement with self-management. This meter rewards proper diabetes management by automatically uploading games onto a portable game system, such as Nintendo DS or Game Boy Advance. Important reasons for using Glucoboy include improving diabetes management compliance, reducing social stigmas linked to diabetes (especially among youth), and changes to child–patient relationships and interactions.

An additional study found that the rewards and reinforcement that video games provide for proper diabetes and general health management habits can improve health outcomes in reality. The improvements to geographic and time constraints in human interactions created by a video game community helps improve interactions with others facing their condition, another advantage found to video game support systems. The ability of video games to serve the purpose of data collection, storage, and goal-setting devices may provide hope for diabetic patients with varying needs.

## Discussion

The financial, societal, and ethical outcomes of self-support technologies on diabetic patients are important. The integration of these perspectives facilitates evaluation of whether these outcomes are positive or negative. The outcomes also are evaluated in the short and long term.

In the short term, there are many financial outcomes from these technologies. They may save diabetic patients time and money from usage, but they may be an expensive investment that cannot be afforded by all. If incorrectly used, some negative and expensive repercussions may result in the short run (e.g., emergency room visits, hospital charges, charges for new equipment if equipment breaks, and more). There also may need to be changes in diet, exercise, and other lifestyle behaviors in order for the technologies to work properly. If these are not adjusted accordingly, the technologies will fail regardless of how useful or potent they may be.

The presence of horizontal and vertical equity that Merson, Black, and Mills (2006, p. 621) suggest applies to self-management technologies. Everyone, regardless of their ability to pay, should have equal access to services and be charged based on ability to pay (p. 622). With technologies, it is difficult to implement this because there are many components to Web-based, mobile, and video game technologies. From the cost of the hardware to the software, there are various parts that go into the cost of the technology, access to the technologies, and possibly risks of geographic isolation from wireless and wired settings. All of these issues may be constraints to using these technologies, depending on an individual's socioeconomic status, health history, and demographic background of the patient.

Another issue is the lack of federal aid. Federal aid has typically been reserved for organizations and settings with patient–provider interaction that use health information technologies, rather than individuals. Examples of individuals receiving self-management technologies are present in the exceptions, such as pilot projects and grants that test technology use on patients and individuals in specific settings and communities. Depending on more patient-centered outcomes research, there is a possibility that federal aid will commit more time, effort, and financial aid toward self-management technologies.

Reasons to expand federal aid to subsidize self-management technologies are numerous. One of the primary reasons for federal aid is to reduce the digital divide by providing free or low-cost technologies to diabetes patients in disadvantaged groups through Medicare or Medicaid. This could have a significant impact, considering that these populations tend to have the highest rates of diabetes and lowest rates of access to preventive care, and no way to report or collect their health information. Secondary reasons include the need for improving the health literacy of the nation through a more informed populace. Merson, Black, and Mills (2006) discuss the role of regulation, but more than likely this will be eased through the PPACA, and focus on government-supported changes and a new focus on a government-regulated health system (p. 654).

Merson, Black, and Mills also suggest the impact on factions/professionals in the technical computer market who produce these goods and who sell to the consumer rather than the health condition (p. 658). This is an important angle, as it suggests both ethical and financial impact on groups who produce these technologies. These groups regulate the quantity of self-management technologies that are supplied and demanded. Yet, over time, these products that were introduced and don't have proper or appropriate impact will be taken off the market. The role of independent research bodies may help regulate the presence of any quackery or spam e-products that don't have a legitimate purpose for diabetic patients. These technologies also will provide substitutes and complements in the markets to telemedicine, telemonitoring devices, e-health, electronic medical records, and other new age technologies.

Some of the longer-term consequences of introduction of such products in the market are changes in federal regulation, such as HIPAA, due to possible impacts on health privacy and security for individuals. While these self-management and self-monitoring technologies are not necessarily compatible or used with other large health systems, they may be, in the future. For this reason, the importance of testing and improvising these systems so they store data safely and efficiently is very important. Having a backup cloud storage for information and also providing safety through password protection will become more important.

Another important finding is that many of the applications created through use of evidence-based clinical guidelines from the National Institutes of Health (NIH) and other agencies still have criteria that is not met. While some major features, such as weight tracking, insulin and glucose level tracking, PHR synchronization, etc., were present, mobile health applications did not place a focus on education. This study also suggested that studies were not conducted regarding the impacts of social media tools in mobile health devices on diabetes management outcomes (Chomutare et al., 2011). Finally, in the long term, Ballegaard (2011) suggests that healthcare technology involves collaboration between patients and the clinician. Health information technology (HIT) is not just a one-way tool used by the patient alone. After using the technologies for mobile self-help aid, some members of the study showed the system to their medical doctor, suggesting that there will be a greater need that will benefit both patients and physicians.

## Conclusion

There are social, political, financial, and ethical policy implications from this chapter. Some of these include relevance to cost savings and saving lives, as well as potential improvements in the general health and health literacy of the nation.

The results of this study suggest that use of such self-management devices, regardless of location, are most effective at educating and motivating populations toward improving their health behaviors. The problem is that many health technology projects are underfunded and may not be targeting the right outcomes. So far, specific interventions—Web-based, mobile phone, and video game—have similar, yet differing, impacts on health outcomes.

The only evidence that was consistent across the different self-management tools was improvements in information gathering and knowledge seeking. Providing tips for self-help on an easily accessible device was one of the most important functions of self-management technologies and served as a benefit in most of the studies. It also suggests that information asymmetries may be reduced through widespread, correct usage of the technologies.

Studies provide contradictory results of various self-management tools on quality of life, nutrition and health behaviors, recording of information, and changes in lifestyle. Web-based interventions (Web sites, e-learning, online portals, digital information) are relatively low cost and easy to use as evidenced by the RCTs that were conducted, but did not suggest striking biological changes (weight, BMI, blood pressure, etc.) for individuals compared to paper-based interventions (novels, guides, pamphlets, brochures, etc.). There was the suggestion that both Web-based and paper-based solutions together had a greater effect than if both were not present in an environment.

Mobile diabetes applications are portable and customer-friendly, but the cost effectiveness is still being debated. Video games are targeting primarily a younger population and may lack purposeful effects after a certain age, though they have grown in popularity. Video games did provide the benefits of improving communication, interaction with other individuals, and positive reinforcement.

The behavioral and social changes that occurred from the technology usage provided the most powerful implications. All the tools provided a social benefit to society, such as improvements in goal setting, reinforcement, and interest toward managing a chronic condition. On the other hand, the technologies inherently have social constraints, such as the digital divide, where many who lack the access to the technology due to socioeconomic or demographic barriers, cannot reach the technologies and, therefore, cannot be impacted through direct technological interventions.

The political implications of the research in the short term may be about who has access to the data collected on patient's self-management from such technologies. The institutions, organizations, and corporations that are creating these tools may have reason to believe they have rights to the data, even though patients are using the tools to store their confidential information. The other issues deal with security and transparency of information, which may depend on the kind of information being received by the patient from the self-management technologies. The long-term implications in the political realm are yet to be explored.

The ethical implications overlap the political implications from the perspective of security, privacy, and confidentiality, and also impact individual rights. The major argument is about the value of a human life, and whether technologies may be destructive to the individual. Lurking questions remain about who is to blame when these self-management technologies are used incorrectly or if the technology itself lacks credibility or benefit.

The literature is primarily inconclusive on whether these tools are actually cost effective for patients. An important finding was that daily usage of such technologies was not providing greater effectiveness and benefits than periodic usage. Some suggestions are that reducing the cost of the applications or devices may provide more incentive for use.

Overall, the study of these technologies only provides motivation for further research. There is much to be explored in the digital age, especially links with patients who have chronic conditions. Due to how recently technology has emerged in self-management of chronic conditions, it is difficult to fully glean the impacts it has had. In the long run, it may be clearer as to the strength of self-management technologies and their positive or negative impacts.

## Limitation of the Chapter and Possible Sources of Bias

Limitations of this chapter include sample size of well-researched papers with strong evidence, the new subject matter, and differences in defining the use of self-management technologies. Sample sizes of literature analyzed in this study were relatively small, making the interventions difficult to generalize. This also reduced the external validity of the studies.

There is a general lack of literature variety, especially mixed methods approaches. Most of the literature involves randomized controlled trials, or RCTs, that test one intervention. Finding studies that test all three types of interventions: video games, mobile health, and online (Web-based) studies is rare, if existent. By including all three types of interventions and then comparing their impacts on one population sample, more analysis may be done on the potency of each intervention and differences in outcomes from the interventions.

Short follow-up periods and personal bias in the survey also may impact the study. Measures of health outcomes are typically nutritional or biological outcomes that are limited in their scope. More health literacy outcomes need to be tested to see how information is reaching audiences and whether this is impacting their actions.

The presence of gray literature and reports are common, whereas meta-analysis from libraries of systematic reviews, such as Cochrane Collaboration, is more limited. Reports show that there is a high demand and supply in the markets, but utilization rate data may be more limited. There also is not enough research across different age and socioeconomic groups. The ethical underpinnings from the technology usage is understated in the literature as well. There needs to be more literature on whether groups of Medicare and Medicaid individuals in pilot studies are able to utilize and benefit from the technologies. This may be of importance during health reform and as Medicaid efforts are being expanded. The usage of such self-management technologies, if beneficial, may be an important supplement to type 2 diabetes treatment.

# References

Arsand, E., N. Tatara, G. østengen, and G. Hartvigsen. 2010. Mobile phone-based self-management tools for type 2 diabetes: The few touch application. *Journal of Diabetes Science and Technology* 4 (2): 328–336.

Ballegaard, S. 2011. *Healthcare technology in the home. Of home patients, family caregivers, and a vase of flowers.* Aarhus, Denmark: Aarhus University, Department of Information and Media Studies, February.

Bird, D., B. Oldenburg, M. Cassimatis, A. Russell, S. Ash, M. D. Courtney, and R. H. Friedman. 2010. Randomised controlled trial of an automated, interactive telephone intervention to improve type 2 diabetes self-management. (Telephone-linked care diabetes project: Study protocol). *BMC Public Health* 10 (1): 599.

Brown, S. J. 1998. Multi-player video game for health education. March 24. Online at: www.google.com/patents/US5730654

Cameron, C., D. Coyle, E. Ur, and S. Klarenbach. 2010. Cost-effectiveness of self-monitoring of blood glucose in patients with type 2 diabetes mellitus managed without insulin. *Canadian Medical Association Journal* 182 (1): 28–34.

Chomutare, T., L. Fernandez-Luque, E. Arsand, and G. Hartvigsen. 2011. Features of mobile diabetes applications: Review of the literature and analysis of current applications compared against evidence-based guidelines. *Journal of Medical Internet Research* 13 (3).

Gee, J. P. 2007. *What video games have to teach us about learning and literacy.* 2nd ed. (revised and updated edition). New York: Macmillan.

Glasgow, R. E., C. T. Orleans, and E. H. Wagner. 2001. Does the chronic care model serve also as a template for improving prevention? *The Milbank Quarterly* 79 (4): iv–v, 579–612.

Kim, C.-J., and D.-H. Kang. 2006. Utility of a web-based intervention for individuals with type 2 diabetes: The impact on physical activity levels and glycemic control. *Computers Informatics Nursing (CIN)* 24 (6): 337–345.

Liebreich, T., R. C. Plotnikoff, K. S. Courneya, and N. Boulé. 2009. Diabetes NetPLAY: A physical activity website and linked email counselling randomized intervention for individuals with type 2 diabetes. *International Journal of Behavioral Nutrition and Physical Activity* 6 (1): 18.

McKay, H. G., D. King, E. G. Eakin, J. R. Seeley, and R. E. Glasgow. 2001. The diabetes network Internet-based physical activity intervention: A randomized pilot study. *Diabetes Care* 24 (8): 1328–1334.

McKay, H. G., R. E. Glasgow, E. G. Feil, S. M. Boles, and M. Barrera Jr. 2002. Internet-based diabetes self-management and support: Initial outcomes from the Diabetes Network project. *Rehabilitation Psychology* 47 (1): 31–48.

Merson, M., R. E. Black, and A. Mills. 2006. *International public health: Diseases, programs, systems and policies.* Sudbury, MA: Jones & Bartlett Learning.

Norris, S. L., M. M. Engelgau, and K. M. Narayan. 2001. Effectiveness of self-management training in type 2 diabetes: A systematic review of randomized controlled trials. *Diabetes Care* 24 (3): 561–587.

Piette, J. D. 2002. Enhancing support via interactive technologies. *Current Diabetes Reports* 2 (2): 160–165.

Ramadas, A., K. F. Quek, C. K. Y. Chan, and B. Oldenburg. 2011. Web-based interventions for the management of type 2 diabetes mellitus: A systematic review of recent evidence. *International Journal of Medical Informatics* 80 (6): 389–405.

*Chapter 5*

# Individualized Prevention Solutions to Childhood Obesity

## Underlying Causes and Consequences of Childhood Obesity

There are a number of factors that impact childhood obesity. The author provides a set of behavioral, environmental, economic, and technological factors and solutions to this important health problem in America today. In the most simplistic sense, childhood obesity is a result of caloric imbalance when calories consumed are greater than those expended (Deghan, Akhtar-Danesh, and Merchant, 2005).

Many a time, individuals tend to say: "I blame it on my genes." To some extent, that is correct. Studies have shown that genetic defects, such as serum leptin, play a role in the development of childhood obesity and/or being clinically termed *overweight* as a child (Zhao and Grant, 2011). Other conditions, such as congenital or acquired hypothalamic abnormalities and various hormone deficiencies, also have been associated with the conditions in children and adolescents (Han, Lawlor, and Kimm, 2010). Yet, this chapter moves beyond the genetic causes of childhood obesity to learn about other factors that may impact the prevalence and prevention of obesity. These other factors may help suggest the sharp rise in obesity rates in the United States in the past few decades (Ebbeling, Pawlak, and Ludwig, 2002).

Physical activity is an important health indicator studied by large government sources of health information, including County Health Rankings, the Behavioral Risk Factor Surveillance System, the U. S. Census, and others. These indicators suggest that physical activity, nutrition, and the presence of sedentary behavior significantly impact adolescents. Consumption of sugar-sweetened beverages may constitute improper nutrition (Ludwig, Peterson, and Gortmaker, 2001; James et al., 2004) through intake of high-calorie snacks, and other processed and packaged foods (Drewnowski and Specter, 2004; Anderson and Butcher, 2006) that may produce imbalances in the diet. To supplement this, sedentary behaviors, such as television viewing, also can lead to a caloric imbalance (Robinson, 2001; Caroli et al., 2004), though less is known about the usage of health technologies and health video games that can actually get the heart rate up and have suggested interesting impacts. These technologies will be discussed more in detail later.

Political tools, such as tax policy, agricultural policy, and food marketing regulations are among the most powerful tools that determine how the land is farmed, what crops are produced at what costs for what price, and who benefits from the production. Current policies encourage large-scale productions of commodities, such as corn, wheat, and soybeans, used in highly processed foods rather than fresh fruits and vegetables. By 2001, the subsidies to these commodities had reached $20 billion per year (Wallinga, 2010).

Economic and political factors have been studied, though evidence remains inconclusive as to how much impact these types of policies have on outcomes (Cawley, 2012). Examples include the price of certain fattening foods and milk, and the demand elasticity that has shown to change differently based on the study. Similarly, BMI (base mass index) has been sensitive to the price of fast foods for lower-income children, reforming agricultural policies will impact availability of many of the ingredients, such as corn, starch, and high carbohydrate vegetables/ingredients in fast-food products.

## Consequences of Childhood Obesity

So, why is it vital to find solutions to the prevention of childhood obesity? The obesity rates have been rising every year and nearly half of Americans may be obese by the year 2030 if the rate of obesity climbs at the current pace. Beyond the numerous health and clinical consequences, obesity drives up costs. Hughes et al. (2012) predicted that the savings in medical expenditures could be much higher if the obesity rate was stabilized than if the rate continues to rise exponentially. Their figures project a savings of $549.5 billion in the next 20 years if the rate remains stable at the year 2010 level. Both childhood obesity and adult obesity are extremely important issues that are closely correlated. Since this chapter focuses on prevention, the author will analyze the root of obesity that can start from a very young age (which is also a compounding problem today) in comparison to regular obesity. The presence of policy interventions are becoming extremely important in curtailing the growth of childhood obesity.

The reason why healthcare spending has increased from childhood obesity is the high cost to produce and sell many pediatric drugs in the market that are supposed to help youth as well as emergency room visit costs and the cost of outpatient and inpatient care (Cawley, 2010).

The development of chronic diseases in younger populations from childhood obesity also can impact life expectancy and has multiple side effects. There are new policy solutions that are present at the individual level for obese children that do not require the level of financial and legislative support that many of the overarching policies have required in the past, thanks to the presence of new technologies, crowdsourcing efforts, and other innovative new solutions. Therefore, research, policies and interventions to prevent childhood obesity are much needed to combat the epidemic (Trasande, 2011).

The next section focuses on policy alternatives for reducing obesity, at the national, state, and local level. These alternatives are assessed by their cost, efficiency, and effectiveness. The assessment is focused on local policies because the level of implementation is easier to achieve at the local level, and it impacts individuals more directly than bills and legislation that are passed at a higher level of analysis. Yet, the author uncovers some of the national and state discussion and policies that have been vital to the study and prevention of childhood obesity.

## National Policy Solutions

A review of the literature suggests that few policies have been enacted (and/or implemented) at the national level for reducing childhood obesity. Many existing policies face barriers in achieving full implementation. There is not enough research to suggest the impact of national policies on childhood obesity, though the author describes some of the policies that have been attempted so far.

The National School Lunch Program (NSLP) provides free or low-cost lunches to schools for children from low-income families. However, Campbell et al. (2011) indicated that many participants in the program are consuming lower-quality diets in comparison to the nonparticipants, while the dietary outcomes between children participating and not participating in the NSLP are not significantly different.

Another policy is the Child Nutrition and WIC Reauthorization Act of 2004, which required all participating schools in the NSLP to establish a local school wellness policy by the first day of the 2006 school year. The wellness policy was to include:

1. Goals for nutrition education, physical activity, and other school-based activities designed to promote student wellness.
2. Nutrition guidelines selected by the local educational agency for foods available on school campus.
3. An assurance that guidelines for reimbursable school meals shall not be less restrictive than federal school meal standards.
4. A plan for measuring implementation of the local wellness policy.
5. Involvement of parents, students, school board, and other interested parties.

However, a study by Brener et al. (2011) found that, among the 538 public school districts that were researched, many schools that have these policies are still not meeting all the elements within the policy.

Another national program is the Head Start Program, established in 1965 under the Head Start Act. This program "promotes school readiness by enhancing the social and cognitive development of children through the provision of educational, health, nutrition, social, and other services to enrolled children and families." The program is supervised by the U.S. Department of Health and Human Services (DHHS), but the program is administered locally by individual preschools. It provides early childhood education to nearly 1 million low-income preschool children. About one in every three children in Head Start is overweight or obese. Hughes et al. (2010) identified barriers in the Head Start Program including lack of time, money, and knowledge, and a cultural belief shared by both parents and staff, which is sometimes inconsistent with preventing obesity.

In addition to barriers in their implementation, difficulties also exist in formulating child obesity-related policies. A major obstacle involves stakeholders and their support. Some studies have suggested the influence of agricultural policy on child obesity (Wallinga, 2010). These studies link the consumption of excess calories from added fats, sugars, refined grains and of snacks, sweets, beverages, and fast foods derived from commodity crops supported under the U.S. "cheap food" policy. Also, the U.S. government requires producers of agricultural commodities, who enjoy such support, to contribute an amount of money into a fund that is used for commodity-specific advertising and research. One of the items that these funds are used to support is the advertising of fast-food menu items (Cawley, 2010).

## State Policy Solutions

State governments have an important role to provide and coordinate funding, collect data for analysis, and regulate practices. State authorities can channel resources to issues and localities that need them most. They have the strongest influence on and the ability to alter community environment by designating land use to accommodate physical activity, building walking and bicycle trails, encouraging safe routes to schools, and regulating fresh produce availability as well as food prices. Obesity-related state regulations in settings, such as schools and child-care facilities, vary greatly from state to state. Some states, such as Tennessee, Delaware, and Indiana, have multiple regulations, such as limiting sugar-sweetened beverages and making drinking water freely available. Other states, such as Idaho, Kansas, and Nebraska, do not have any obesity-related regulations (Benjamin et al., 2008).

# Local Policy Solutions

To document local alternatives, a set of systematic reviews were analyzed to group information and classify the importance of each of the reviews and their findings. From the scan of the literature, it was found that a number of different local initiatives have an impact on childhood obesity. The following section details a list of environmental, economic, behavioral, political, and technological initiatives at the local level that impact childhood obesity.

The biggest difference in interventions is whether it is focused on prevention or treatment. This study focuses on prevention-based alternatives, which are also the same direction that health reform and current health policies are moving toward. Treatment-based interventions have not provided clear results on effectiveness or long-term consequences. For this reason, the author provides a number of evidence-based articles, using systematic reviews, to develop the policy options that may counter childhood obesity issues today. These policies focus exclusively on prevention interventions because even the most recent drug-use randomized trials to treat obesity in children show unconvincing impacts on body mass index, with no evidence for long-term maintenance as well as side effects, such as significant gastrointestinal adverse effects (Viner et al., 2010). Medications and lifestyle interventions may work, though, in the long run, they again may not provide the strongest or most effective results (McGovern et al., 2008). Policy interventions remain the focus of the literature scan, as these have the greatest effect on the community.

It is likely that local-level institutions, agencies, schools, and other stakeholders have an effect on the community, which is why policy interventions that target the various stakeholders are a part of the study. The following is a range of environmental, economic, political, and technological policies that could have an impact on childhood obesity issues.

## Environmental Policies

The first two environmental local initiatives involve changing the proximity to fast-food outlets for individuals in a community, especially for individuals in low-income neighborhoods, and potential changes to nutrition menu labeling. Yet, many available studies indicate no effect from changing the proximity to fast-food outlets, and some effect from nutrition labeling, though changing labels on food products is a long process that is difficult to implement in the short term. By identifying environmental alternatives that include an analysis of location of unhealthy food in proximity to major childhood activities, including community centers, churches, schools, etc., it may be useful to understand the impact of unhealthy fast-food restaurants, vending machines, social media, education, and raising awareness through improved parenting. Reducing sedentary behaviors also are important, which can be accomplished by increasing the availability of parks and recreational activities in the neighborhood, while reducing unsafe behaviors, gangs, and criminal activities in a community, which tend to jeopardize children's interest in the outdoors.

A number of local government committees (2009) discuss the following as local priorities: zoning restrictions on fast-food restaurants near schools and playgrounds, community policing to improve safety around public recreational sites, limiting video game and TV time at publicly run after-school programs, and taxing high-calorie, low-nutrient foods and drinks (Committee on Local Obesity Prevention for Local Governments et al., 2009). These are some of the strategies local governments can use to combat the problem. For example, in 2010, Congress passed the Healthy, Hunger-Free Kids Act (Sec. 204 of P.L. 111-296) and added new provisions for local wellness policies related to implementation, evaluation, and publicly reporting on progress of local wellness policies. The effects of this are yet to be seen.

The presence of local zoning policies have been assessed by Chen and Florax (2010). Their study analyzed how zoning policies that impact chain groceries, in turn, can influence access to healthy foods in disadvantaged neighborhoods and BMI of children in the neighborhoods. Using spatial policy simulation and GIS (geographic information system) techniques, this study found the health effectiveness of an increase in access to (and number of) grocery stores within close proximity to disadvantaged neighborhoods. There was a statistically significant impact from an increase in grocery stories on BMI ($p < 0.05$). Topics relating to geographic disparity will be discussed in greater detail in Chapter 9.

## Physicians and Health Providers

Friedman and Schwartz (2008) discusses some of the low-cost, obesity prevention high-impact strategies that can be used by physicians, such as: outreach to local, state, and federal government; opinion as outreach to local, state, and federal government; opinion posting in blogs and Web sites on policy issues; speaking at public meetings; writing policy endorsements in various media portals; working and voting for legislative initiatives to prevent childhood obesity, and more. Health providers are now being held more accountable for their actions through health reform. Changes to reporting standards of tax benefits by nonprofits and for-profit hospitals require the presence of community health needs assessments, which represent allocation of community benefit and programs that involve the community's health needs.

At the individual level, there is a lot that can be done. Some examples include healthy eating and lifestyle changes, breast-feeding, increasing physical activity, drinking water, and media/social networks. These examples may vary in terms of feasibility and effectiveness for different groups of people due to issues of access and usage. While these are not all easy to achieve or cost effective, schools, parents, and the community can work together to improve health outcomes through a combination of these tactics.

## Media Impacts

Haby et al. (2006) analyzed effectiveness of 13 obesity prevention programs on body mass index (BMI) units saved and disability-adjusted life years (DALYs) saved in Australia. They found the most health benefits and effectiveness from a reduction of TV advertising of high fat and/or high sugar foods and drinks to children, laparoscopic adjustable gastric banding, and the school programs that involved an active physical education component. Analyzing these results, all outcomes can be fairly expensive, as different stakeholders must share in the changes. For example, media may take a loss from reduced TV advertising, though it could make it up by advertising less sugary, healthier drinks. Gastric banding after a certain age may be feasible for those in advantaged classes, unless it is subsidized locally. School programs require funding to achieve an active physical education component in the school day. Harvard School's The CHOICES (Childhood Obesity Intervention Cost Effectiveness Study) three-year project will closely mirror this Australian example. Also, collaborating for these purposes may be made difficult due to the political constraints, discussed next.

The President's Council on Physical Fitness and Sports is developing a Fit 'n Active Kids Program. The Partnership for a Walkable America is an extensive public–private collaboration to promote walking and improve conditions for walking. The America on the Move initiative sponsored by the Partnership to Promote Healthy Eating and Active Living (an organization of nonprofit and private-sector partners) targets prevention of adult weight gain as a first step toward combating obesity; the initiative specifically advocates increasing physical activity by 100 calories per day and decreasing caloric intake by 100 calories per day. The Centers for Disease Control and Prevention's

(CDC) VERB campaign focuses on media messages on physical activity for 9- to 13-year-olds and involves collaborations with schools, youth organizations, and other organizations.

Farm-to-school initiatives also can provide important impacts. For example, in Texas, the Interagency Farm-to-School Coordination Task Force has representatives from TDA, TEA, the Texas Department of State Health Services (DSHS) and other groups. Others who take part include parents, school food services, agriculture, nutrition and health educators and researchers, and fruit and vegetable producers and distributors. This initiative has the following functions: to "create a database of food producers by locale, assist farmers and ranchers with marketing their goods to schools, and design and update nutrition and food education resource," according to Susan Combs, Texas comptroller of public accounts.

## Economic Policies

The economics of childhood obesity, especially at the local or individual level, are still unclear, and may have varying effects according to state policies, local policies, and demographics within neighborhoods. This can limit researchers from drawing important conclusions. Some of these unknowns include externalities, such as diet-related diseases and losses in productivity, information asymmetry (proper information gathering and information spreading) regarding unhealthy eating habits and behaviors, and revenue generation. So far, studies have focused on the amount of revenues that have poured in by levying taxes on specific foods. For example, sugary beverage sales have been documented in New York, where an extra penny tax can produce nearly $1.2 billion in revenue, while being found to reduce consumption nearly 10%, as proposed by Brownell and Freiden (2009). Taxation is a political issue as well that could be highly debated across the country, and can vary by locality and state because many states do not believe that taxing individuals for eating foods of their choice is a fair or reasonable transaction.

Another interesting way to assess economic policies on obesity is to understand the presence and changes to school-based programs on healthy eating. For example, Flodmark, Marcus, and Britton (2006) conducted a systematic review analyzing school-based programs, studying 24 cases of prevention-based interventions on childhood obesity, before and after a 12-month period for normal or high-risk populations. The outcomes were body mass index (BMI), skinfold thickness, or the percentage of overweight/obesity that were tested before and after the studies. Of the 24 studies analyzed, 15 studies reported that prevention alternatives had a statistically significant positive effect on obesity, while the remainder reported neutral results and none reported a negative result at a $p < 0.00$. Nearly half of the studies showed a positive effect from prevention at the $p <. 00$ level of significance.

The affordability of healthy foods, which is an economic issue, is a major problem for disadvantaged populations. For this reason, the pricing and consumption of unhealthy foods must be analyzed more closely. Brownell and Frieden (2009) discuss the impacts of taxes on sugary beverages. There has been a 30% increase in per capita impact of consumption of sugary beverages, which has gone above healthier options, such as milk. Yale University's Rudd Center for Food Policy and Obesity completed a review on sugary beverages that suggested that for every 10% increase in price, consumption decreased by 7.8%. Brownell and Frieden (2009) reported that as prices of carbonated soft drinks increased by 6.8%, the demand elasticity was easily affected, so consumption patterns sales dropped by 7.8%; similarly, as Coca-Cola prices increased by 12%, sales dropped by 14.6%. A tax on sugary beverages may influence elasticity, including choices between unhealthy and healthy options toward sugary beverages and whether or not individuals may decide to switch to cheaper alternatives because their current options have risen in price.

Congress allocated new funds in the recent Agriculture Appropriations bill passed in October 2012. Department of Agriculture officials fast-tracked the release of new regulations to guide the implementation of the new money by the states. The money was available immediately; states had until April 30, 2013 to begin distributing funds. For Fiscal Year 2014, the Senate Appropriations Committee and Agriculture Appropriations Subcommittee marked up their agriculture spending bill which allocates $20.93 billion in funding for agriculture, rural development, nutrition and food safety programs to begin on October 1st. Due to the discrepancy in funding, which is nearly $420 million higher than the current enacted levels, there may be some problems in matching the funding to the House's agricultural bill. The House allocation estimate is close to $1.5 billion less than the Senate version (National Sustainable Agricultural Coalition, 2013). To supplement these efforts, crowdfunding and crowdsourcing may be options to provide funding for public campaigns and legislative support for conservation programs, rural development and farm loans, and research and education on nutrition in agricultural programs.

Examples of specific states that have taxes on unhealthy foods are listed in the Yale Rudd Food Policy Report (2012). This list below includes state excise tax and sales taxes, though studies have shown that sales tax is typically more effective.

Hawaii: Bill number S.B. 2480—$0.01 per teaspoon of added sugar

Illinois: Bill number S.B. 396—$0.01 per ounce; revenues toward Illinois Health Promotion Fund

Mississippi: Bill Number S.B. 2642—$2.56 per gallon of sweetened beverage produced or $0.02; 20% of revenue would go to Children's Health Promotion Fund

Vermont: H.B. 615—$0.01 per ounce; revenue would be used to create Vermont Oral Health Improvement Fund

The Brookings Institute also came to some conclusions on childhood obesity. Children covered by Medicaid are nearly six times more likely to be treated for a diagnosis of obesity than children covered by private insurance. Children treated for obesity are roughly three times more expensive for the health system than the average insured child. Annual health-care costs are about $6,700 for children treated for obesity covered by Medicaid and about $3,700 for obese children with private insurance. The national cost of childhood obesity is estimated at approximately $11 billion for children with private insurance and $3 billion for those with Medicaid. Children diagnosed with obesity are two to three times more likely to be hospitalized. Children who receive Medicaid are less likely to visit the doctor and more likely to enter the hospital than comparable children with private insurance. Children treated for obesity are far more likely to be diagnosed with mental health disorders or bone and joint disorders than nonobese children.

## Political Community Relationships/Partnerships

Krishnaswami et al. (2012) looked at community engagement in child obesity interventions. Their results found that there are positive effects of community engagement on achieving child obesity intervention outcomes. They also found that the impacts of community engagement differ by school–community partnership—groups engaging in "community/academic entity" or "administrator" showed positive correlation. Thus, they concluded that greater school–community partnership can facilitate obesity prevention intervention to achieve more weight-, diet-, and activity-related outcomes.

Many of these studies show the short-term effects on treatments for obesity, rather than long-term projections and impacts. This could be something that needs greater study and funding by policy programs and policy analysis.

Local nonprofit organizations, such as youth organizations, faith-based groups, social and civic organizations, and ethnic organizations, have an important role in combating childhood obesity. Many of these organizations already have an interest in improving the well-being of members of their community through initiatives such as those aimed at reducing alcohol consumption, smoking, and driving under the influence. These entities can use their connections with the locals and their experience implementing related programs in addressing the childhood obesity epidemic. In addition, public/private partnerships with these organizations targeting at-risk populations also present great potential. In recent years, new organizations have been formed in various localities with the mission to reverse the obesity trend. For example, ProActive Kids (PAK) Foundation in Illinois, formed in 2009, partners with healthcare providers in offering nutrition consultation and exercise programs that are free to physician-referred participants. Choosing Healthy & Active Lifestyles for Kids (CHALK) is another collaboration between New York Presbyterian Hospital and the local community to promote creating an environment for and the culture of healthy living.

The principles of social entrepreneurship have been widely utilized to create social change in the past decade. This, too, is a powerful channel through which the nonprofits can address childhood obesity. Ashoka United States (Arlington, VA) is an example of a nonprofit organization that supports social entrepreneurs who combine economic principles with social goals to solve pressing problems of their local communities. Currently, Propeller is a project to deliver healthier school lunches to children in New Orleans through a reform of school food contracting processes. The project also brings economic opportunities to local farmers as participating vendors are required to shop locally. Local nonprofits are partnering with Propeller to monitor food quality, participation rates, and stakeholders' attitudes in the program.

Corporations in the private sector also are important stake-holders. They are the ones with financial resources to support or initiate various projects. Many companies now have a nonprofit arm to which part of the proceeds from the for-profit entity is channeled to support various causes. This is not merely an act of giving away. Corporate philanthropy is often viewed as cause-related marketing (Ross et al., 1992). There is evidence that firms that engage in corporate philanthropy have higher expected future revenue (Lev, Petrovits, and Radhakrishnan, 2010). The insurance industry, in particular, can directly benefit from healthy lifestyles. These firms should be encouraged to contribute.

In the next 20 years, nonprofit organizations are likely to become more powerful and capable of effectively and efficiently addressing the issue of childhood obesity. The nonprofit sector has been growing quickly and steadily in the past decade. According to the Urban Institute (Washington, D.C.), between 2001 and 2011, the sector grew more rapidly than both the business and government sectors, increasing the number of nonprofits by 25%. Local nonprofits have the advantage of having cultural knowledge of the community in which they are located and, thus, are able to tailor interventions to the needs of the members. The concept of social entrepreneurship within the nonprofit sector also should be exploited as it promotes sustainability and empowerment of the locals.

Veugelers et al. (2005) analyzed schools with and without nutrition programs and schools following the Annapolis Valley Health Promoting Schools Project (AVHPSP) (Nova Scotia, Canada) that used CDC recommendations for school-based healthy eating programs. Veugelers et al. (2009) found that students in schools from AVHPSP had healthier habits, lower rates of obesity, and were more prone to be a part of physical activities. General nutrition programs (that weren't AVHPSP) didn't make a significant difference on the schools, though AVHPSP did. This helps us conclude that more research on the guidelines provided by AVHPSP is needed, so that policy makers can use programs similar to the AVHPSP program all over the country.

## Child Care Policies

Considering the importance of preschool years to childhood obesity prevention, Larson et al. (2011) reviewed literature on state regulations, practices and policies, and childhood obesity interventions on children at child care centers. The authors found that in terms of child care settings, most states lack strong regulation on healthy eating and physical activity. Many state regulations on physical activity and playground safety do not comply with national health and safety standards. Reviewing current policies and practices related to childhood obesity prevention and at child care centers, Larson et al. suggest that future efforts should be made to improve nutritional quality of food provided at child care, increase the time children are engaged in physical activity, and offer health education at child care and through caregivers.

Focusing on nutrition policies and the impact of caregivers on children at child care centers, Erinosho et al. (2012) studied 50 child care centers in North Carolina. They found results with clinical significance that caregivers were observed modeling healthy dietary behaviors more often at centers with written policies about staff modeling and health eating, discouraging unhealthy foods for meals and snacks, and having informal nutrition talks at meals. Child care centers may play an especially large role on the American family lifestyle, because there is higher dependence on child care in the United States and western countries more so than eastern countries. This phenomenon places a fairly important responsibility in the hands of child care centers to be motivating, encouraging, and modeling a healthy diet and active lifestyle for the children who attend the centers.

## Technological Policies and Social Media

Use of Web 2.0 technologies, including electronic health tools as discussed in Chapter 4, as well as social media, may be an interesting new solution to childhood obesity intervention and as a form of prevention. Believing that these new communication technologies allow an innovative, participatory communication environment, many health practitioners and researchers have been conducting studies on the impacts of these technologies on shaping health knowledge, attitudes, and behavior (Chou et al., 2009). Such studies include computer and Internet programs for smoking cessation (Chen et al., 2010), food safety education (Bramlett Mayer and Harrison, 2012), mental health (O'Dea and Campbell, 2011), pediatric type 1 diabetes (Franklin et al., 2006), and sexual health (Moreno et al., 2009) where positive effects on health improvement are found by implementing these programs.

In recent years, Internet- and social media-based health promotions have been explored by practitioners and researchers on childhood obesity studies. Compared to traditional schemes, utilizing the Internet and social media can offer children individualized intervention and prevention schemes that are tailored to their background, age, gender, socioeconomic status, etc. The programs can include interactive, self-paced health education programs, self-monitoring of food, weight and activity, individualized feedback and counseling, and also individualized education targeting children's parents. Systematic reviews have shown that Web-based programs could impact children in terms of healthy eating and physical activity (An et al., 2009).

The intervention and prevention programs also can take advantage of the pervasive social media technologies. With social media, children can share their health knowledge and experience with their friends, search for and provide support with other obese children, and be motivated by competitive and interactive games, exercises, or other incentives delivered over the social media. More importantly, as more children are involved in the programs, we can expect the growing positive effect in the social network—that children are influenced by their friends who have made healthy eating and physical activity moves. Not enough pilot studies have been conducted to suggest just how serious the cost effectiveness and quality of health benefits are when including social media as part of one's lifestyle. Theoretically, interventions based on subjects' social networks are congruent with early findings that individuals' health can be affected by their social networks (Smith and Christakis, 2008; Langlie 1977), so that these networks could be leveraged for obesity intervention and prevention. The recent report by the American Heart Association evaluated studies on social media to suggest the effectiveness on children's health. The study found that the frequency of logging into and using such programs, coupled with family involvement and peer support, as well as mentoring and open communication about the obesity prevention or treatment program using social media, was a strong approach (Li et al., 2013).

An important challenge in the use of social media and Internet technologies in childhood obesity is the digital divide because its presence across America affects access to and use of the Internet and other electronic technologies among the population. The discussion of geographic disparities in healthcare (especially based on technology usage and health literacy) have been covered somewhat in Chapter 2, and will be the focus of Chapter 9 as well. The divide is strongly associated with demographic characteristics of individuals, which can be blamed on history, culture, health knowledge, and health access and availability in different parts of the country as well as around the globe. This is especially apparent when comparing across rural and urban American consumers, patients, and providers. Chapters 6 and 7 explore the differences across rural and urban health providers in their experiences with technology. Also, studies have indicated that the divide parallels the pattern of health disparities in many ways because such inequalities have been found in health information technology adoption across different socioeconomic groups and health literacy levels (Chou et al. 2009), not to mention the strong association between childhood obesity and their socioeconomic status. Therefore, policies addressing the use of the Internet and social media on childhood obesity should consider providing incentives and support to children from low-income, low-education, ethnic, and rural families.

Telehealth, in the form of teleconferencing, is known to provide relationships between providers and those in need of healthcare for childhood obesity and other conditions in geographically disparate areas. Believing that these new health technologies allow for an innovative, participatory communication environment, many health practitioners and researchers have been conducting studies on the impacts of these technologies in shaping health knowledge, attitudes, and behavior (Chou et al., 2009). Such studies include computer and Internet programs for smoking cessation (Chen et al., 2012), food safety education (Bramlett Mayer and Harrison, 2012), mental health (O'Dea and Campbell, 2011), pediatric type 1 diabetes (Franklin et al., 2006), emotional well-being (Gay et al., 2011), and sexual health (Moreno, 2009), where positive effects on health improvement are found by implementing these programs.

## *Political Impacts*

A report by the Office of the State Comptroller provides suggestions on how local, state, and national government action works together in making positive change a reality. Many managed care plans are more likely to cover obesity and weight management programs/issues in 2010 than they were in 2008, a sign that health reform and health insurance expansion may help reduce obesity. The USDA's Expanded Food and Nutrition Education Program (EFNEP) combines resources of county Cooperative Extension System services and other local agencies to reach low-income families and youth. While New York school districts must meet guidelines on school lunch menus, there were no restrictions on other foods, including vending machine purchases. After the completion of audits, the problem of high levels of unhealthy foods were being sold was found to exist and exacerbating childhood obesity. For example, New York City schools were found to be selling high amounts of junk food, candy, and soda, known as "competitive foods," but after audits and restrictions that suggested no selling of these foods after lunch period, there was a reduction in the amount of unhealthy foods being bought.

The CATCH initiative, started by the Center for Healthy Living at the University of Texas School of Public Health's Austin campus, was created "to promote physical activity, healthy food choices, and to prevent tobacco use in elementary school-aged children." This study also has been analyzed for cost effectiveness with returns of $889.68 for every dollar invested, as measured by "the extension of quality years of life and the avoidance of $68,125 in future healthcare costs for each participant" (http://www.window.state.tx.us/specialrpt/obesitycost/preface.php).

## Conclusion

Childhood obesity can be impacted by a variety of environmental, economic, political, and technological solutions as depicted by the examples provided above. The author has grouped a number of studies and provided impacts suggested by these studies and potential solutions for individuals and families in producing improved health outcomes targeting childhood obesity. The environmental solutions include big picture strategies, such as national- and state-level legislation that must be enacted, such as safer neighborhoods, better zoning policies, and improved afterschool programs and school policies toward food and physical activity, while local solutions include all of these solutions, as well as local level food chains and farmers' markets that can improve the quality of food provided to the community as well as social entrepreneurship at a grassroots level. The media can have its role in depicting a particular prevention tool as positive or negative and creating a bias on the audience as to the usability of that particular strategy. Economic solutions include national- and state-level policies on taxation and subsidies for certain foods that impact elasticity. Technological solutions include social media and electronic health options, crowdsourcing, and telehealth, which may improve the quality of healthcare received across regions, with long-term cost effectiveness as well. Finally, the political solutions offered include improving coordination and collaboration across various stakeholders so that information is more easily integrated across databases, and communication channels are properly being navigated to get patient information from one health provider to another. These solutions discussed have had interesting outcomes so far, though more research will provide some of the shortcomings and areas needing improvement.

# References

Anderson , P., and Butcher, K. (2006). Childhood obesity: trends and potential causes. *Future Child*, 16(1), 19–45. HYPERLINK "http://www.ncbi.nlm.nih.gov/pubmed/16532657" \t "_blank" http://www.ncbi.nlm.nih.gov/pubmed/16532657

Benjamin, S. E., Cradock, A., Walker, E. M., Slining, M., and Gillman, M. W. (2008). Obesity prevention in child care: A review of U.S. state regulations. *BMC Public Health*, 8(1), 188. doi:10.1186/1471-2458-8-188

Brener, N. D., J. F. Chriqui, T. P. O'Toole, M. B. Schwartz, and T. McManus. 2011. Establishing a baseline measure of school wellness-related policies implemented in a nationally representative sample of school districts. *Journal of the American Dietetic Association* 111 (6): 894–901.

Brownell, K. D., and T. R. Frieden. 2009. Ounces of prevention—The public policy case for taxes on sugared beverages. *New England Journal of Medicine* 360 (18): 1805–1808.

Campbell, B. L., R. M. Nayga, J. L. Park, and A. Silva. 2011. Does the National School Lunch Program improve children's dietary outcomes? *American Journal of Agricultural Economics* 93 (4): 1099–1130.

Caroli, M., L. Argentieri, M. Cardone, and A. Masi. 2004. Role of television in childhood obesity prevention. *International Journal of Obesity and Related Metabolic Disorders: Journal of the International Association for the Study of Obesity* 28 (Suppl 3): S104–108.

Chen, S. E., and R. J. G. M. Florax. 2010. Zoning for health: The obesity epidemic and opportunities for local policy intervention. *The Journal of Nutrition* 140 (6): 1181S–1184S.

Chou, W. S., Y. M. Hunt, E. B. Beckjord, R. P. Moser, and B. W. Hesse. 2009. Social media use in the United States: Implications for health communication. *Journal of Medical Internet Research* 11 (4): e48.

Deghan, M., N. Akhtar-Danesh, and A. T. Merchant. 2005. Childhood obesity, prevalence and prevention. *Nutrition Journal* 4 (1): 24.

Drewnowski, A., and S. E. Specter. 2004. Poverty and obesity: The role of energy density and energy costs. *The American Journal of Clinical Nutrition* 79 (1): 6–16.

Ebbeling, C. B., D. B. Pawlak, and D. S. Ludwig. 2002. Childhood obesity: Public-health crisis, common sense cure. *Lancet* 360 (9331): 473–482.

Erinosho, T. O., D. P. Hales, C. P. McWilliams, J. Emunah, and D. S. Ward. 2012. Nutrition policies at child-care centers and impact on role modeling of healthy eating behaviors of caregivers. *Journal of the Academy of Nutrition and Dietetics* 112 (1): 119–124.

Flodmark, C.-E., C. Marcus, and M. Britton. 2006. Interventions to prevent obesity in children and adolescents: A systematic literature review. *International Journal of Obesity* 30 (4): 579–589.

Franklin, V. L., A. Waller, C. Pagliari, and S. A. Greene. 2006. A randomized controlled trial of Sweet Talk, a text-messaging system to support young people with diabetes. *Diabetic Medicine: A Journal of the British Diabetic Association* 23 (12): 1332–1338.

Haby, M. M., T. Vos, R. Carter, M. Moodie, A. Markwick, A. Magnus, A., ... B. Swinburn. 2006. A new approach to assessing the health benefit from obesity interventions in children and adolescents: The assessing cost-effectiveness in obesity project. *International Journal of Obesity (2005)* 30 (10): 1463–1475.

Han, J. C., D. A. Lawlor, and S. Y. S. Kimm. 2010. Childhood obesity–2010: Progress and challenges. *Lancet* 375 (9727): 1737–1748.

Hughes, C. C., R. A. Gooze, D. M. Finkelstein, and R. C. Whitaker. 2010. Barriers to obesity prevention in Head Start. *Health Affairs* (Project Hope) 29 (3): 454–462.

James, J., P. Thomas, D. Cavan, and D. Kerr. 2004. Preventing childhood obesity by reducing consumption of carbonated drinks: Cluster randomised controlled trial. *BMJ* (Clinical Research Ed.) 328 (7450): 1237.

Krishnaswami, J., M. Martinson, P. Wakimoto, and A. Anglemeyer. 2012. Community-engaged interventions on diet, activity, and weight outcomes in U.S. schools: A systematic review. *American Journal of Preventive Medicine* 43 (1): 81–91.

Langlie, J. K. 1977. Social networks, health beliefs, and preventive health behavior. *Journal of Health and Social Behavior* 18 (3): 244.

Larson, N., D. S. Ward, S. B. Neelon, and M. Story. 2011. What role can child-care settings play in obesity prevention? A review of the evidence and call for research efforts. *Journal of the American Dietetic Association* 111 (9): 1343–1362.

Lev, B., C. Petrovits, and S. Radhakrishnan. 2010. Is doing good for you? How corporate charitable contributions enhance revenue growth. *Strategic Management Journal* 31 (2): 182–200.

Li, J. S., T. A. Barnett, E. Goodman, R. C. Wasserman, and A. R. Kemper. 2013. Approaches to the prevention and management of childhood obesity: The role of social networks and the use of social media and related electronic technologies: A scientific statement from the American Heart Association. *Circulation* 127 (2): 260–267.

Ludwig, D. S., K. E. Peterson, and S. L. Gortmaker. 2001. Relation between consumption of sugar-sweetened drinks and childhood obesity: a prospective, observational analysis. *Lancet* 357 (9255): 505–508.

McGovern, L., J. N. Johnson, R. Paulo, A. Hettinger, V. Singhal, C. Kamath, … V. M. Montori. 2008. Clinical review: Treatment of pediatric obesity: A systematic review and meta-analysis of randomized trials. *The Journal of Clinical Endocrinology and Metabolism* 93 (12): 4600–4605.

Moreno, M. A., M. R. Parks, F. J. Zimmerman, T. E. Brito, and D. A. Christakis. 2009. Display of health risk behaviors on MySpace by adolescents: Prevalence and associations. *Archives of Pediatrics & Adolescent Medicine* 163 (1): 27–34.

National Sustainable Agricultural Coalition. (2013, June). Retrieved 2013, from  HYPERLINK "http://sustainableagriculture.net/blog/senate-ag-approps-2014-bill/" \t "_blank" http://sustainableagriculture.net/blog/senate-ag-approps-2014-bill/

O'Dea, B., and A. Campbell. 2011. Healthy connections: Online social networks and their potential for peer support. *Studies in Health Technology and Informatics* 168, 133–140.

Parker, L., A. Burns, and E. Sanchez. 2009. Local government actions to prevent childhood obesity. Online at: http://www.nap.edu/openbook.php?record_id = 12674 (accessed December 30, 2012).

Robinson, T. N. 2001. Television viewing and childhood obesity. *Pediatric Clinics of North America* 48 (4): 1017–1025.

Smith, K. P., and N. A. Christakis. 2008. Social networks and health. *Annual Review of Sociology* 34 (1): 405–429.

Teufel-Shone, N., Fitzgerald, C., Teufel-Shone, L., and Gamber, M. (2009). Systematic Review of Physical Activity Interventions Implemented with American Indian and Alaska Native Populations in the United States and Canada. *American Journal of Health Promotion* ,23(6), S8–32. doi: HYPERLINK "http://dx.doi.org/doi:%2010.4278/ajhp.07053151" doi: 10.4278/ajhp.07053151

Trasande, L. (2011). Quantifying the economic consequences of childhood obesity and potential benefits of interventions. *Expert Review of Pharmacoeconomics & Outcomes Research*, 11(1), 47–50. doi:10.1586/erp.10.86

Van den Berg, M. H., Schoones, J. W., and Vliet Vlieland, Theodora. (2007). Internet-Based Physical Activity Interventions: A Systematic Review of the Literature, *Journal of Medical Internet Research*, 9(3), :e26. Retrieved from  HYPERLINK "http://www.jmir.org/2007/3/e26/" http://www.jmir.org/2007/3/e26/

Veugelers, P. J., and Fitzgerald, A. L. (2005). Effectiveness of School Programs in Preventing Childhood Obesity: A Multilevel Comparison, *Am J Public Health* 95(3), 432–435.

Veugelers, P. J., J. D. Fisk, M. G. Brown, K. Stadnyk, I. S. Sketris, T. J. Murray, and V. Bhan. 2009. Disease progression among multiple sclerosis patients before and during a disease-modifying drug program: a longitudinal population-based evaluation. *Multiple Sclerosis* (Houndmills, Basingstoke, England) 15 (11): 1286–1294.

Viner, R. M., Y. Hsia, T. Tomsic, and I. C. K. Wong. 2010. Efficacy and safety of anti-obesity drugs in children and adolescents: Systematic review and meta-analysis. *Obesity Reviews: An Official Journal of the International Association for the Study of Obesity* 11 (8): 593–602.

Wallinga, J. 2010. From walls to windows: Using barriers as pathways to insightful solutions. *The Journal of Creative Behavior* 44 (3): 143–167.

Zhao, J., and S. F. A. Grant. 2011. Genetics of childhood obesity. *Journal of Obesity* 2011, 845148.

# Suggested Readings

American Public Health Association (APHA). n.d. Fighting childhood obesity through local policy. Online at: http://www.apha.org/membergroups/newsletters/sectionnewsletters/comm/spring09/fightingobesity.htm (accessed December 30, 2012).

Amis, J. M., P. M. Wright, B. Dyson, J. M. Vardaman, and H. Ferry. 2012. Implementing childhood obesity policy in a new educational environment: the cases of Mississippi and Tennessee. *American Journal of Public Health* 102 (7): 1406–1413.

Cawley, J., and C. Meyerhoefer 2012. The medical care costs of obesity: An instrumental variables approach. *Journal of Health Economics* 31 (1): 219–230.

Centers for Disease Control and Prevention (CDC). n.d. NPAO—Local school wellness policy—Adolescent and school health. Online at: http://www.cdc.gov/healthyyouth/npao/wellness.htm (accessed December 30, 2012).

Centers for Disease Control and Prevention (CDC). n.d. Policy resources: Overweight and obesity. DNPAO. Online at: http://www.cdc.gov/nccdphp/DNPAO/policy/obesity.html (accessed December 30, 2012).

Collins, C. E., J. Warren, N. Neve, P. McCoy, and B. J. Stokes. 2006. Measuring effectiveness of dietetic interventions in child obesity: A systematic review of randomized trials. *Archives of Pediatrics & Adolescent Medicine* 160 (9): 906–922.

Daniels, S. R., M. S. Jacobson, B. W. McCrindle, R. H. Eckel, B. M. Sanner. 2009. American Heart Association childhood obesity research summit executive summary. *Circulation* 119 (15): 2114–2123.

Koplan, J. P., C. T. Liverman, and V. I. Kraak. (eds.) 2005. *A national public health priority*. Institute of Medicine (US) Committee on Prevention of Obesity in Children and Youth. Online at: http://www.ncbi.nlm.nih.gov/books/NBK83827/ (accessed January 14, 2013).

Leung, M. M., A. Agaronov, K. Grytsenko, and M.-C. Yeh. 2012. Intervening to reduce sedentary behaviors and childhood obesity among school-age youth: A systematic review of randomized trials. *Journal of Obesity* 2012, 1–14.

Marder, W., and S. Chang 2005. *Thomson Medstat brief: Childhood obesity*. Ann Arbor, MI: Thomson Medstat.

McVey, G., J. Gusella, S. Tweed, and M. Ferrari. 2008. A controlled evaluation of Web-based training for teachers and public health practitioners on the prevention of eating disorders. *Eating Disorders* 17 (1): 1–26.

National Academies Press (NAP). n.d. Progress in preventing childhood obesity: How do we measure up? Online at: http://www.nap.edu/openbook.php?record_id=11722&page=111 (accessed January 13, 2013).

National Center for Biotechnology Information. n.d. The economic impact of obesity in the United States. Online at: http://www.ncbi.nlm.nih.gov/pmc/articles/PMC3047996/ (accessed January 30, 2013).

National Institute for Health and Care Excellence (NICE). n.d. Preventing obesity—A whole-system approach: Call for evidence. Online at http://www.nice.org.uk/guidance/index.jsp?action = folder&o = 48269 (accessed December 30, 2012).

Parker, L., A. Burns, and E. Sanchez. n.d. Local government actions to prevent childhood obesity. Online at: http://www.nap.edu/openbook.php?record_id = 12674 (accessed December 30, 2012).

Paxson, C. H., E. Donahue, C. T. Orleans, and J. A. Grisso. 2006. Introducing the issue. *The Future of Children* 16 (1): 3–17.

Powell, L. M., J. F. Chriqui, T. Khan, R. Wada, and F. J. Chaloupka. 2013. Assessing the potential effectiveness of food and beverage taxes and subsidies for improving public health: A systematic review of prices, demand and body weight outcomes. *Obesity Reviews* 14 (2): 110–128.

Ross-Degnan, D., S. B. Soumerai, E. E. Fortess, J. H. Gurwitz. 1993. Examining product risk in context: Market withdrawal of zomepirac as a case study. *JAMA* 270 (16): 1937–1942.

Thow, A. M., S. Jan, S. Leeder, and B. Swinburn. 2010. The effect of fiscal policy on diet, obesity and chronic disease: A systematic review. *Bulletin of the World Health Organization* 88 (8): 609–614.

Wolfenden, L., J. Wiggers, E. Tursan d'Espaignet, and A. C. Bell. 2010. How useful are systematic reviews of child obesity interventions? *Obesity Reviews: An Official Journal of the International Association for the Study of Obesity* 11 (2): 159–165.

# NATIONAL AND INTERNATIONAL IMPACTS OF HIT ON THE COMMUNITY

IV

## Chapter 6

# Health Information Technology in Community Health Centers

## *Chapter Summary*

This chapter provides an example case study and research design for the topic of community health centers (CHCs). It is an important discussion due to the lack of projects studying the issue. Community health centers are institutions that were created by the federal government in the late 1970s to improve access to quality healthcare in underserved and underfunded areas. Due to healthcare reform and changes to healthcare since the technology boom in the early 2000s, CHCs are being developed and expanded. They seem to have produced beneficial care for the Medicaid, Medicare, and uninsured communities. This also can generate healthcare savings for the taxpayers who fund these programs. To ensure their continued efficiency and effectiveness, it's important to analyze CHCs and generate reasoning for their productivity. Past literature focuses on either the technological or managerial contributions that have made improvements to the quality of care and cost at CHCs. Factors, such as health information technology (through training and usage of electronic medical records (EMRs)) and community involvement and funding (through the written Community Health Needs Assessment (CHNA) process), provide improvements to CHCs can make a difference on the U.S. healthcare framework at large.

# The Formation of Community Health Centers (CHCs)

The growth, development, and investment in CHCs for uninsured and underserved populations has emerged as a trend since the passage of the Affordable Care Act (ACA) and U.S. healthcare reform of 2009. These clinics, also known as federally qualified health centers (FQHCs), for rural and impoverished medically underserved areas (MUAs) and medically underserved populations (MUPs) have been around since the late 1980s, but were not used nearly as frequently and stagnated in their development for the past two decades. Finally, since the early 2000s, they have been developing because the government decided to invest more in the CHCs due to a sudden surge in the demand for their usage. Possible reasoning for increases in this demand is the new importance placed on healthcare reform as well as healthcare information technology in various acts: Health Information Privacy Act (HIPAA), Health Information Technology Act (HITECH), etc. There was interest starting in the latter Clinton term, and continued through the investment in CHCs in the Bush era. Then there was a strong healthcare reform pursuit during the

Obama administration to build on these centers due to the growing uninsured populations, especially in rural areas, who needed access to care at low cost or possibly at no cost. There is importance in usage of CHCs for preventative and primary care, especially among the poor, so that the expensive emergency room usage can be reduced and early access to treatment and cures can be provided rather than treatment that requires lengthy hospitalization and inpatient care. Overall, early access to care can reduce mortality rates, improve the quality of life for many of the poor, and reduce costs across the board, both for the federal government and for the individual who uses tremendous resources in the healthcare system.

So, how are CHCs established and what specific resources do they provide? CHCs are grant funded, meaning it is a competitive process to apply for funds to operate the CHCs and dependency persists on the local, state, and federal government in receiving aid for operation. Because of this process, CHCs differ from other nonprofit hospitals as well as for-profit hospitals, because they depend on strong networks and relationships with organizations and funders in the community as well as from the government and state. The CHCs that thrive have a larger investment of capital due to influential board members who can drive change and provide the resources necessary to improvise the structure.

CHCs are especially important because access to hospitals and larger facilities may be many counties away for those in rural areas and too expensive for impoverished communities. Therefore, CHCs can provide care for various programs, such as primary care, oral and dental care services, counseling, maternal health, health and sex education, psychiatry and mental health, drug prevention/rehab, and more. The programs can really benefit if individuals begin using these facilities early on so that they can deduce illness or diseases early on, and begin treatment rather than holding off until it's too late. Many of the programs also are not just for treatment, but for mental and behavioral programs, providing help to those with mental disorders, obesity prevention, pregnancy care, etc. These are the kinds of programs that provide nurturing as well as increased awareness and education to populations that don't have great access to multimedia, technology, television, and/or transportation to travel to large cities. Because they are not as connected to the outside world and may not be cognizant of what is going on and what healthcare needs they should be fulfilling, from immunizations to disorders, it provides a strong support system, which is the reason CHCs are being pushed to the forefront today.

Interestingly enough, there is still work to do during the growth of CHCs, as they are catering to some specific populations that vary by race, ethnicity, gender, etc., based on the region they are in. For example, Ohio continues to have a large white majority, more than 90%, at CHCs, but the Hispanic population has been growing over the years, so language barriers that can be overcome through usage of electronic medical records in the clinics may be extremely important. New techniques must be developed so that the evolution of CHCs continues to progress in the right direction as the kinds of population accessing care continue to grow and change. Currently, almost two thirds of CHCs/FQHCs' patients are racial minorities, and 9 out of every 10 individuals have incomes well below the poverty line (200% of the federal poverty line). Those with no health insurance at CHCs are at a ratio of 4 in every 10 individuals. The dynamic of the number without health insurance versus those who may need Medicaid will change drastically when the individual mandate becomes effective requiring healthcare to be purchased by every individual. For this reason, this is one of the new angles targeted by this study to see changes in pre- and post-healthcare reform populations that will improve their quality of care and cost effectiveness, as a patient's insurance status changes.

The focus on both the community and the technology that is invested in CHCs is important and not covered previously by the literature. For this reason, it is important to focus on both of these characteristics, though the primary hypothesis is based on technology impacting CHCs. It is a possibility that Community Health Needs Assessment (CHNA) reports also are driving change in CHCs because of their goal-oriented nature and the requirement that CHCs look to the community to tailor their programs. This is important because the dollars spent on new programs should be invested with diversification and on the programs most in need for each specific county, be it obesity prevention in Cuyahoga County, Ohio, or out-patient care facilities to the Mormon-populated communities in Ashland County, Ohio. At the same time, it is important to measure the progress made by technology at health centers because, over time, progress can increase, stagnate, or even be decreasing if technology is not used correctly. In this study, the phrase HIT use is defined in many contexts, including technology training programs for staff to learn how to use EMRs, quality improvement programs that test interoperability and usage of technology, frequency of technology usage across multiple departments (including radiology, pediatrics, psychiatry, e-prescribing) as well as across clinics and institutions to support faster care and decrease duplication of x-rays, lab tests, records of treatment, and other data.

## Theory for the Design

As shown, there is a rising need to study the impact of the CHCs on the rural and impoverished patients they are serving to study whether cost effectiveness and healthcare quality objectives are reached. Today, nearly 1 of every 19 people living in the United States now relies on a federally funded clinic for primary care and 40% of these are uninsured and one-third are children (Shi and Singh, 2004). The newest studies on the subject cover two different perspectives on how CHCs are achieving the goals of cost effectiveness and improved patient quality of care. The theories state that either health information technology (HIT) or a strong political agenda is driving change. This study questions how the Community Health Center (CHC) framework is improving its patients' quality of care while managing cost effectiveness, looking at pre- and post-healthcare reform periods and changes in insurance coverage for those attending CHCs. The study adds to past bodies of literature by targeting the period before and after the ACA to see how CHCs are catering to a rising uninsured and Medicaid patient base, as well as looking at numerous methods of change including technology and CHNA write-ups that provide a goal-setting aspect.

A few different theories will be able to explain the changes to the CHC infrastructure during the nation's healthcare reform. Due to the HITECH Act, which is a part of the ACA, there has been a growth in use of technology in the hospital and community health center setting. Technology diffusion is a key socioeconomic and scientific theory to changes in how CHCs have undergone development. It is rooted in change theory, which states that there are particular steps that the staff in clinics undergo—precontemplation, contemplation, preparation, action, and maintenance—before completely accepting and implementing technology into the workplace and the technology taking effect. Building a wider knowledge and skills base through use of HIT and quality improvement programs are an incremental approach because they slowly build on the current state of the clinic and may cause greater change in the long run over the short run. The first hypothesis for this theory is that, as HIT and Quality Improvement (QI) intervention programs are used to train staff so that they are better equipped to handle the technology and assess the departments that need focus, it contributes to a higher state of care and cost effectiveness. Operating technology in CHCs contributes to higher productivity because studies have shown that CHCs that use HIT tend to have patients with lower rates of hospital readmissions, greater screenings for early onset diseases, and lower ambulatory care service (ACS) discharge rates versus other smaller clinics (Shields et al., 2007). HIT also provides for early identification of illness and reduces the duplication of tests (and x-rays) that would normally contribute to the cost of a patient's checkup.

Another important hypothesis of technology enhancement is that increasing technology in CHCs ensures easy coordination and access to each other's facilities, which, in turn, increases the quality of care and lowers the cost. Going along with this has been studies about "innovation networks" and how coordination among facilities would better the CHC's functioning as well (Carroll et al., 2010). This part of the hypothesis focuses on electronic health records (EHRs), which connect clinics to other clinics and other hospitals so that rapid results can be generated with easy collaboration between regions, not just organization-wide change, which would suggest need for an EMR. Quick prevention and rapid response is crucial in the healthcare industry during a generation of disease and trends that impact the community on a global level. By fulfilling multiple goals, such as better infrastructure through improved coordination networks, well-trained staff, and improved medical error rates, as well as lower costs to the overall healthcare system in the long run, HIT diffusion and innovation seems to be a plausible theory for the improved state of CHCs. An alternate theory, or organizational behavior management, pulls from Chester Barnard's* works on organizational behavior and management in major policy decisions to explain how health reform impacts every level of government. This will be used in the framework of this alternate theory by suggesting that the community, local leaders, and organizational behavior characteristics, if monitored frequently, may drive responsibility within the community toward achieving help for the disadvantaged and disabled. There is a hint of altruism and socioeconomic theory to this alternative theory because it is a combination of efforts from the local community involvement and the internal management of the CHCs that together impact change. Examples of the impact of community efforts led by management and the community input are both prevention and behavioral health programs, such as obesity prevention, alcohol abuse, mental health, and more, which are then documented in the CHNAs. The use of these reports then will provide a way for clinics to analyze which areas of the community are lacking and which are improving, so that reduced hospital usage will occur and better preventive measures will be taken in the community. This is also a good way to set goals and track trends in the community so that again there is greater cost effectiveness toward the necessary initiatives and improved patient quality of care.

Two hypotheses from this theory are:

1. A rise in altruism in the community, nonprofit doctors, and trained staff within the organization as well as incidence of town hall meetings, fundraising projects, and a philanthropic society contributes to the improved CHCs after the ACA.
2. Population health management objectives and goal setting through the CHNA process and better alignment of community programs with community needs will provide a mechanism to analyze the community and allocate money into the right pockets of need.

It is assumed that with a more altruistic environment of leadership, commitment, and overtime work from staff, and community involvement activities, such as increased town hall meetings and fundraising for the health centers, the most cost-effective solutions and quality of care occur. It will be interesting to test whether electronic medical records and quality improvement standards are the true root of the improvement in quality care for the uninsured or if it's the foundation of community altruism and organizational behavior that is contributing to the changes in the CHC framework. Population health management is a new movement focusing on objectives, goal setting, and benchmarks to suggest and drive comparisons that promote improved outcomes for quality of care. The possibility exists that there is some interaction between these components that causes the improved state of CHCs and this will be tested as well to provide articulate solutions, something that has not been done in previous studies.

The dependent variables in this study are:

1. Quality of care that will be measured by certain characteristics (vaccination rates, screening rates, reduced ACS discharge rates, an acute care treatment rate, and an aggregate quality improvement score).
2. Cost effectiveness, measured by Medicaid claims savings from the years pre- and post-ACA reform, cost savings per person based on HIT pre- and post-ACA legislation, and cost per month per person to the uninsured pre- and post-ACA.

These will be the ways to test whether or not the study has been able to achieve the priorities of efficiency and effectiveness, especially from a surge in federal funding toward the CHCs. The unit of analysis is the patient because the quality of care and cost effectiveness define the patient's healthcare situation.

For the first theory in the study, which is in regards to HIT and how HIT has an impact on quality of care standards, the CHCs in the study will be compared to CHCs without HIT. The CHCs should be randomly sampled from the entire group of CHCs in one region of the country. Keeping within one region will standardize the region for geographic factors that may impact patients from being very different in conditions to each other. For example, the prevalence of diabetes may be much higher in Dallas, TX, than New York City, so it's better to compare the CHCs in the South with each other than to do cross-regional comparison on diabetes work. The hypothesis generated from the study assumes that with HIT, CHCs will be more cost effective and provide better measures of quality care. For example, ACS discharges (unnecessary hospitalization rate) at CHCs with HIT should be lower for those with high blood pressure due to diabetes, compared to those at CHCs without HIT. The HIT will be a component of quality improvement programs, where staff is better trained on new, efficient methods to handle data collection, technology implementation and usage, patient interaction, and more. The mechanism causing the improvement in quality of care are these quality improvement programs, which will be under a pretest posttest format. The way it has been done in many studies is to include a quality improvement score to see how a CHC does, based on a group of criteria. This mechanism of testing for quality improvement and ranking of EMR implementation and usage has been used by many studies in a variety of different fields. Providing a goal-oriented and scored logic to the study provides for easier understanding of the characteristics where the CHC is lacking and where more work needs to be done. This also provides trends for areas of improvement in technology diffusion.

The alternative theory to this study assumes that organizational leadership and goal setting for the community in CHCs are what lead to their improvements in quality of care and cost. The comparison group is still other CHCs in this theory. In quantitative terms, measurements will be derived from a score based on criteria found in the CHNA report data given to the CHCs to collect. The CHNAs will include information, such as budgetary amounts of fundraising, amount of charitable donations to the organization, fundraising for the uninsured, etc. The second hypothesis from this theory is that increased state and local funding through donations and championing new efforts toward healthcare will increase quality and decrease costs. Senators and congressional representatives may champion a specific ACA-funding policy to improve the condition and number of mental, behavioral, or primary care CHCs in their districts. So, here, lobbying efforts and voting behavior pre- and post-ACA reform for CHCs and efforts toward health policy can be measured. Besides an empirical analysis of community and state fundraising within the CHCs, leadership characteristics will be measured through surveys and focus groups to observe how the CHC leaders feel they are altruistically improving their infrastructure. These theories differ because the first theory discusses how HIT and quality improvement standards have socioeconomic impacts on CHCs through technology growth, whereas the second theory raises the issue of political consequences, both within a structure and the political climate surrounding it, that may be impacting the structure.

Some of the rationale for the strength in the HIT diffusion theory outweighs the probability that altruistic leadership and pluralist theory alone is driving change. Because these health centers are nonprofit and of a charitable nature, it's much harder for them to be influenced by political funding because political figures cannot get a great deal of clout from making decisions on a nonprofit organization. On the other hand, if these centers were structured and taxed like corporations (that fund their own research for cures and have a political voice), they could speak to the heart of the political matter and be impacted significantly by the political aspects of the government. The predicted shortfall of doctors and trainees in healthcare also leads to unanswered questions on how to fill this void at nonprofit clinics, like the CHCs, that are not providing any incentive for doctors to practice there. Again, this makes for a better case for technology to be at play, because technology can be a driver in revamping institutions from the ground up and also be an assistance during shortages of healthcare personnel including physicians, nurses, and more. The best way to compare the theory to its alternative would be to test HIT on CHCs that are focused on specific issues, such as diabetes. Since such an issue can be seen as a political "hot potato" or topic that congressional representatives and senators are afraid to get too close to, it may be easier to disprove that organizational behavior/political leadership theory impacts CHCs compared to the logic that HIT impacts a specific illness's outcome. The HIT theory of using quality improvement training programs is more generalized to varying health and preexisting conditions for patients at CHCs that bolster external validity. The political theory may only impact select CHCs in select regions where political dogma supports the efforts of a specific illness or health condition.

## Literature Review

Looking at past literature, there are various mechanisms derived to test the theories that are proposed in this chapter. Authors have tested health information technology at clinics, how technology impacts the status of quality of care for chronic condition patients, and specific technological improvements, such as QI programs that are driving change within CHCs. To test the other theory and hypothesis, some literature covers organizational behavior within CHCs through survey research to analyze how organizational behavior impacts CHCs. Since the CHNA reports are a concept that is currently being proposed to become mandated and most CHCs have not had a tracking mechanism for this, these are not discussed in any literature. For this reason, CHNA reports and testing their significance in driving change is a must for this chapter. So, much of the literature focuses on technological change and some of the community aspects, but parts of the theory driven in this chapter, such as CHNA reports, are new and not covered in past works.

Organizational behavior studies are the first focus of literature that has been done. Studies take different angles in the analysis. While some studies focus on the functionality of the organization, such as its cost structure and ability to run on low revenue, other studies focus on the management and leadership characteristics within the organization. Gusmano, Fairbrother, and Park (2002) analyze the specific services that CHCs do a good job of treating, with a focus on the uninsured. Categories, such as primary care and general medication, supplies, etc., are compared to services that are lacking, typically behavioral and specialty care. More research has been done since this work was published on these specialty care services and is covered next. The study brings out an interesting point. The institution must serve its patients regardless of ability to pay, which means it can write off the cost of the visit as bad debt or provide alternative sources of payment plans and fee schedules to accommodate their client base. Fundraising and community/state giving also will play an important role in providing funding for such centers in picking up the slack that patients can't afford.

This means organizational behavior characteristics and the community giving theory will govern studies like this. Physicians also may feel less incentive for serving their clientele, especially those in after-hours care with low reimbursement. Thus, improvising on goal-setting mechanisms, through CHNAs (that have not been tested in past literature) and use of technology may be the best substitute in the future if there are shortages of doctors. Incorporating interviews with the directors of the CHCs and asking them key questions on funding and care also generate findings on motives for improving care or cost. Yet, surveys may not be as conclusive as secondary data stating quality of care objectives achieved, or data from records.

Literature discussing community health centers with specific chronic care patients, such as improvements in quality of care for diabetes centers, mental health centers, etc., is another interesting way to analyze CHCs. Lishner and Richardson (1996) do a thorough literature review on CHCs that treat for disabilities care. It provides a good history of CHCs and how care for disabilities can be studied through qualitative analysis. This study may be difficult to prove causally and may lack external validity throughout. It maintains the theory that better training and personnel may be needed for such varying kinds of care (diabetes versus asthma, etc.). It also concluded that areas with low-income populations are most susceptible to problems like obesity and, in turn, diabetes, mental problems, and other preexisting conditions. Building on this, a study on chronic disease at CHCs for those with diabetes, hypertension, and asthma by Landon et al. (2007) introduce a valuable research design, with a strong pretest–posttest component of CHCs undergoing the quality improvement tactics. Its comparison group is of CHCs that had not engaged in such QI training programs. Disease treatment, prevention, screening, and monitoring went through improvements through the study. By representing CHCs in various parts of the country, the study depicts external validity. Yet, being that such a study uses internal targets for individual centers (i.e., centers assess themselves and provide goals of quality improvements), it's much more difficult to be sure that the measures are all based on similar criteria, especially if centers are targeting different health conditions. The structure of the research design is randomized, so it eliminates some of the common bias and internal validity problems. While the literature is thorough, an addition to studies on chronic care patients may be through goal setting of CHNAs.

Another work that focuses on the literature of chronic disease care is Hicks et al. (2006), who look at quality of care from a different angle—how the uninsured versus the insured are treated at CHCs. This was an interesting study and shares similar characteristics with the Landon et al. (2007) article. It administers intervention programs in a quasi-experimental design, with an equal proportion of centers from the geographic regions in the United States rather than conducting it in a randomized format. These quality improvement intervention programs are tested for benefits to CHCs in quality of care standards, specifically treating for diabetes, asthma, and hypertension issues over time. Greater foot exams and hemoglobin control among diabetes patients as well as dilated eye exams and lipid controls, were examples of improvements through QI training (Hicks et al.. 2006, pp. 1721–1722), EMRs were the format for only about 41% of the CHCs, and were used in incorporating the results of the quality of care findings. A new addition to the study was organizational characteristics. The organizational behavior, management, and other criteria were presented in a survey and the results were then correlated with the quality of care results to see what specific organizational criteria impacted the quality of care data. Some of the interesting developments that can be tested further are the difference in older CHCs and rural health clinics (RHCs) (built over 30 years ago) and how they differ from those today that have better infrastructure, technology, and other features. The study also states that computerized decision support actually positively impacted frequency of care, benefiting new CHCs, but has not done any in-depth analysis of HIT.

A study by DeVoe et al., (2011) recorded differences in Medicaid claims and EMR data of 50 CHCs in Oregon, shedding light on how EMR usage differs from Medicaid claims, and the policy impact on record keeping. EMRs had a beneficial impact on recording data of populations of "discontinuously uninsured," potentially improving the documentation of quality of care provided in comparison to Medicaid claims. EMR usage and, in turn, features of HIT impacts the CHC client base. This provides more information on how to measure data on a certain patient base—the uninsured, those above the federal poverty level, and Spanish speakers—because these individuals cannot be tracked through Medicaid claims data alone, and may be left out in many studies that use only Medicaid claims. The study is focused more deeply on the theory of measurement of data that can be improved through HIT and QI, rather than intervention programs' effects on CHCs using a scoring mechanism for quality of care. These theories differ in their logic and approach of improving technology standards at CHCs in order to improve care, with a focus on specific kind of patients who visit CHCs. This study by DeVoe et al. (2011) also sheds light on how coordination between EMR systems is key in the new age because the transfer of data and comparative effectiveness research can be conducted in a smoother manner. This study is specific to Oregon and diabetes care, which, at best, will be generalizable for other CHCs or RHCs in the Midwest. It leaves out the importance of affordability of EMRs as a large investment that is pertinent to CHCs. Similarly, a study by Carroll et al. (2010) discusses the importance of "innovation networks." Coordination through innovation networks are the glue between healthcare providers as well as between academic institutions and providers by providing stronger links to bolster research usage and access.

Chin et al. (2000) discuss the measurement of *adherence* to quality, or testing how closely CHCs follow guidelines for administering care. They found that 55 Midwestern diabetes CHCs had low rates of adherence. Another study by Chin et al. (2007) also suggests the importance of quality improvements through political engagements, including coordination/ collaboration efforts (like disparity collaboratives) that may cause CHCs to have increased adherence to standards and regulations. Thus, the suggested research design includes political impacts on CHCs. Proser (2005) and Proser et al. (2011) discuss the positive outcomes of CHCs on quality of care, cost effectiveness, and comparisons between CHCs and primary care. Outcomes specific to improvements in hospital service usage through CHC presence are suggested by Rothkopf et al. (2011). Such themes could be tested to suggest the impact that HIT has on QI interventions and adherence at CHCs, in comparison to other sources of primary care. From a cost standpoint, Ku et al. (2009) participated in a federally funded initiative to measure both out-of-pocket expenditures and ambulatory care expenditures at CHCs. They found that expenditures were lower for patients participating in CHCs. Also piggybacking on this, McRae et al. (2006) focus on cost effectiveness for adults over 18 with a category for disabled versus not. This study also found that users of the CHCs paid about $400 less per month than non-CHC users. Similarly, Duggar et al. (1993) discussed that total per person Medicaid payments were 33% less for CHC members in California, along with 38 percent lower inpatient hospital admission rates.

Finally, there is literature on how CHCs and other government centers, such as the RHCs for the impoverished, differ. Rather than grouping all health centers together, a HRSA study focuses on how a rural health clinic may differ from one that has an emphasis on a federally defined "poor" population. Some interesting characteristics of health centers include comparisons of their scope of services (HRSA, 2006, p. 13), management, and leadership (p. 17), and financial backing (p. 30). Having a pharmacy, after-hours care, and dental and primary care for all ages are not a necessity for rural health clinics, though they are for CHCs. Some services also are only covered under Medicare or Medicaid, which can be specific to community or RHCs. Sliding fee scales are not necessary in a RHC, though a board of directors is, and independent audits are not required for RHCs and CHCs do require these services. The way they are treated even from a tax and governance standpoint may impact how RHCs versus CHCs function and deliver quality care to patients because there may be more at stake to lose or gain from a healthcare transaction. These differences may make for an interesting study, also trying to analyze why more RHCs are trying to convert to CHCs and what the strengths and weaknesses are between them. RHCs also can serve as a strong comparison group for a study on CHCs in terms of level of technological development that each have and the input necessary for the future.

State funding typically goes into decline during periods of economic unrest and recessions, so the community giving and leadership theory may be lacking. Since 2004, the United States has had a hard time with finding the means to fund both federal and state projects, which may impact a quality care and cost effectiveness study. Data as recent as 2010 show that out of 33 states that provide funding for health centers (grouped as a conglomerate of all kinds of health centers), 23 states have reduced their funding toward community health centers, 7 increased funding, and 7 remained at a status quo. California was the most impacted state, and had to close down six centers and lose 170,000 patients in the process (McKinney et al., 2010,

p. 3). Because capital is not a major focus of federal funding, states must pick up the differential and contribute more in the infrastructure and capital arena to compensate for growth of CHCs, which needs more focus today. Also important will be to watch for changes to CHCs due to a growing population that will see new Medicaid enrollees through expanded Medicaid coverage and the Individual Mandate provision requiring purchase of individual health insurance nationally. This study has a domestic focus, incorporating literature on different components of the U.S.'s CHCs, and hopes to contribute to further research improvising on past studies.

## Research Design

Next, the author provides an example of a strong research design to test the research question. Two important components will create a strong research design in analyzing the progress that CHCs have had during healthcare reform. The first project will be focused on qualitative observations, through a randomized experimental design, while the second project will be a survey research design that can be analyzed with a strong quantitative component as well as an unstructured interview section for observation and qualitative findings. Together, these components complement each other by providing internal and external validity that can bolster the study with a combination of the two types of projects. Whereas a randomized study typically generates a high level of internal validity, its ability to be applicable to larger populations can be difficult and not as reasonable. It is difficult to relate a group of participants participating in a randomized trial and then expect them to continue attending the same clinics as they did in the study because it may not be feasible based on their living conditions in reality. On the other hand, a study that is a survey provides some interesting feedback that can be objective and subjective. It has the ability to be applicable to the public because it identifies major issues and focus areas for the participants with a fairly large number in the study and a spread of groups, such as the directors, physician, and patients all participating. But, internal validity can be a concern because of the way interviews are structured and biases generated during presentation, within the survey questions and during analysis of the observations. While statistical analysis may bolster a causation relationship in the study, the statistics can be merely probabilistic, which allows for weaknesses to warp the study. For this reason, an open-ended component to the survey allows for more in-depth answers and/or comments that may supplement a purely statistically computed set of questions.

## Research Experiment 1: Randomized Experimental Design

The author continues with a discussion of two example research experiments. What makes this research experiment interesting and unique in its research design is its factorial randomized experimental design format. Typically, studies have incorporated either political or scientific factors into this literature, and tested that as the independent variable that could be impacting the dependent variable, outcomes relating to the CHC's patients. This study targets *both* political and scientific factors as potentially important independent variables and can vary the level of subdivision of each factor. This reduces the possibility of confounding factors and experimental error. The real disadvantages of such a study is that a high level of precision is required and there's an inability to measure more than two key independent variables.

This study will test two major independent variables: (1) community intervention variables based on community health needs assessments administered, and (2) presence of HIT and other electronic techniques that scientifically impact the CHCs through quality intervention training programs, electronic medical records, etc. In this study, the unit of analysis is the community health center, because the focus is of contributions to the improvement in the health center and then to the patient. It is based on the theory that there are community-driven efforts as well as a scientific rationale at varying levels that better society. There is not much literature on the interaction of the community encompassing variables, such as community health needs assessment reports, that health centers and hospitals should be providing every two to three years, to assess community issues, concerns in their impact on the CHC framework, and, in turn, patient quality of care and cost. These reports are important in identifying the nature of problems or strengths in a community where more funding and progress should be directed, and target political and state leadership components (access to resources, transportation, disease, religious issues) that have impact on the community's access to healthcare. Furthermore, they can access the changes to the insurance status of a population, so that greater efforts to capture a movement toward Medicare or Medicaid may be seen now that the Individual Mandate clause of health reform passes. For this reason, the community variable will be one important, independent variable, because it is testing whether the impact of these reports can individually affect cost and quality of care because of its goal-oriented nature and an early needs-based perception. The second independent variable is HIT, measured through the aggregate of a scoring system of dummy variables: the impact of quality intervention training programs to implement the technology, use of electronic medical records, use of e-prescriptions, and use of HIT both between CHCs and between CHCs and hospitals. The blocking variable will be a weighted score of both the community variable and HIT to see whether the two together may have an impact on the patients.

Looking at operationalizing this design, about 100 CHCs in regions in the Midwest with no technology will be selected. They will then be separated into two categories: (1) 50 of those who will get the effects of technology intervention and (2) 50 who will not be administered the technology to write the community health needs assessment reports. The logic of starting these centers on the technology from scratch is to identify any change or intervention effect without the effects of "history" (an internal validity issue) in the experiment. Being a double blind experiment, patients also will not know whether they are randomly attending a CHC with technology and CHNA reports or one without them. Patients will either be assigned to attend a CHC with the technology and reports or be in the control group without them, for a two-year period, with an incentive of all co-pay and transportation for visits paid for by the study. Being a pretest posttest factorial design, both the control group and variable group of patients will be measured before attending the community health center to judge their perception of quality of care and how much they pay in healthcare typically measured in dollar amount per year, possibly further delineated by Medicaid amount, co-pay, etc.

Next, each of the patients will begin using the CHC and continue services through that center, either in the CHC with intervention variables or in the control group at the CHC without them. Some overall controls in both groups worth mentioning are: factors for state leadership, such as how much a state has provided for funding its CHCs; political leadership at the state level (providing sophisticated CHC growth efforts through financial contributions, community hall meetings, and campaigns and bills passed in support of CHCs); and the number of CHCs that are currently open and running in that state. Also, federal-level grants and funding will be controlled so they don't influence the results. These are important characteristics that may vary in a specific region, thus, holding them constant so they don't intervene in the experiment is important.

The independent variable measuring community intervention will have a score derived by the presence of community health needs assessments, which are reports done at the county level. These community needs assessments are not required of the county, but are expected of hospitals, from a new PPACA (Patient Protection and Affordable Care Act) regulation. It would be important to test to see if they are required and what effect they have on the care. These will only be reports conducted by the intervention group (not the control group). The community variable will be scored on the content of the needs assessment, based on what needs the community has in terms of funding, illness, and more, and the usefulness of the assessment to physicians and community stakeholders. The technology variable will have a score, but it will be derived through characteristics, such as use of different kinds of health information technology—electronic medical records, electronic prescriptions, electronic charts; use of HIT from one CHC to the next; the different departments of the center (whether none, some, or all) that are using the technology; and presence of quality training programs to implement the technology. Based on these aggregate variable scores, as well as the interaction term that is a combination of these variables, there should be an impact on the dependent variables, including cost effectiveness and healthcare quality. The best way to measure the dependent variable of cost effectiveness is to see the change on the patient's cost of care, based on charge for follow ups (which are typically more expensive without technology, with a need for a duplicate x-ray, records, etc.) before and after the intervention both from CHC care and possibly reduced need for hospital admissions, measured by the amount paid in emergency room expenditures, and amount of money spent for days at the hospital. The healthcare quality can be measured by the ambulatory discharge rate (or number of preventable discharges), patient satisfaction of the healthcare center, immunization rates, and the rate of medical errors measured postintervention. Sampling problems in the study may include correlation of the characteristics in the scoring of the variables, and finding the best way to weigh and factor the various variables, because this is key in the factorial design.

One of the most important factors in the study is time. The time variable is the backdrop, which will precipitate causation in the study. Because this is a randomized study, there is no need for pretest posttest measures. Having a before time/after format and the passage of time does strengthen the study's internal validity because of the sensitivity of the variables. Both the implementation of technology and the fact that this study is conducted before and after healthcare reform legislation makes the time factor crucial. For this reason, a two-year period, from 2011 to 2013, is decided upon between the pretest and posttest measurements.

On the other hand, this presence of time contributes to one of the weaknesses that there can be in the study. Maturation and history of patients in the study impact outcomes, because of an extended period of time, and with patients whose illnesses change or progressively worsen. To placate problems, the study will incorporate patients who are primarily attending with no preexisting conditions or diseases and have been using CHCs for primary care across one region, such as the Midwest. This will prevent other errors from seeping in, especially that of sampling. There must be many demographic controls in the study, including patient race, sex, age, family history of conditions, insurance, and others, such as population density and proximity to a hospital, in order to standardize the patients who attend the health centers. External validity is a greater threat than internal validity. The study is difficult to carry out in real-world contexts because CHCs develop at different rates and may not all be technologically progressive at the same rate, based on geographic, population, and other outside factors, which makes the design less representative. Yet, CHCs are controlled and standardized so that they can be analyzed from the perspective of any region's CHCs once this format is tested.

Finally, after tracking at six-month intervals and the passage of a two-year period, the impacted group will be compared to the comparison group. If the technology has not had a justifiable and statistically significant impact on the community health centers, and the centers still have presence of cost effectiveness and healthcare quality improvements, this means that the impact is primarily due to the community reports' variable, based on the scoring initiatives. On the other hand, if there has been a statistically significant impact by the technology, the measures of cost and quality of care will be improved, and the community variable may not be significant. Last, if the blocking variable measuring both shows statistical significance, then both variables have had an impact. The hypothesis is that the impacted group will generate cost savings and healthcare quality improvements under the technology's impact.

The final report for this component of the project will provide a vivid picture of the experiment's findings and have many dimensions. The randomized design provides a gold standard for the study, and strengthens internal validity. Yet, the flaws that may still persist include interaction effects between selection bias and the experimental variable, generalizability to an experimental setting over a nonexperimental setting, and multiple treatment interference. This is where controlling for the effects of each of the independent variables may be at jeopardy since the design is factorial and across various units and subunits. Yet, the strengths of the study justify the causal nature of the study. This study gets to the heart of the issue impacting CHCs' patients by measuring impacts of both technology and community emphasis on healthcare. By encouraging the community to be involved and also providing technological progress, there should be enhanced benefits derived by the nature of healthcare in a rural and underserved population.

## Research Experiment 2: The Survey Design

The survey design method will have its own shortcomings and strengths, being that data may be objectively tested through a quantitative mechanism using specific survey questions and subjectively driven by opinions and perspectives from respondents. It can help supplement a randomized experiment through improved external validity.

The chosen survey research design for this project will involve a multinomial logistic regression research method technique. The survey will generate responses on a Likert scale, based on responses of 0 (disagree strongly) to 5 (strongly agree). The study will be a set of surveys, with two essential parts. The first part has survey questions that are scaled, documenting changes to essential characteristics in the CHCs and discussing impacts of technology in the CHCs. The second part of the survey will be the open-ended testaments of participants, especially components that patients feel were not included in the survey. Some of the major factors taken into account when creating the survey design are (1) proper treatment of the target population, (2) ease of communication tools (in-person, mail, phone) in asking questions, (3) respondents' willingness and incentive to participate, and (4) response accuracy.

For this study, there will be three groups responding to the survey, with different methods of approach. The three groups include directors and organizers of the CHCs, physicians at the CHCs, and the patients at CHCs. Being both a longitudinal design and panel data, the groups will be identified preintervention (pretechnology) and then postintervention (two years later) and, this way, the exact same respondents will be providing responses, reducing some of the effects of history in the internal validity. The format for the directors and physicians will be phone interviews and mail-in questionnaires, whereas patients will be part of a focus group as well as the mail-in questionnaire, with an incentive for completing the survey—a small cash payment. The focus group (in-person) format for the patients will provide a better observational study and some evidence of changes that occur that may be indirectly or directly related to the intervention. On the other hand, phone interviews are conducted for directors and respondents due to ease of access and ability to get in touch with directors who may not be at the clinic setting all of the time. The survey questions will be written and tailored to each of the three groups' function in the healthcare system, so that the interviewees can shed insider insight.

The number of respondents in the CHCs will total 100. This will be broken down into 20 directors of various CHCs in a state, 30 physicians of the same CHCs, and then 50 patients attending and willing to continue attending the same CHCs for a two-year period. Sampling will be done through an interesting process, as the category of respondents will be notified differently for participation. The respondents from the director and physician groups will be randomly selected for the call process through access to an online database and cold calling the major primary clinics to see who is interested. This is publicly available data. On the other hand, due to confidentiality restrictions from the new HIPAA laws, access to the private listing of patients attending CHCs may be denied, so the best method to find out patients visiting CHCs is self-selection. When patients attend the CHCs, they will be asked whether they want to participate in the survey and focus group, and will provide contact info, their e-mail and mailing addresses. If they sign up, they will be provided a $25 cash incentive as well. Once the quota for the number of patients needed in the survey is reached, the selection process is closed.

Postsurvey weighting also will help balance any sampling bias, by adjusting for characteristics of the region, such as number of clinics in the region for the county and the female versus male respondents, as well as income, race, and other demographic and socioeconomic differences between respondents. The survey methods will be identically administered across three states in the Midwest and compared: Indiana, Ohio, and Illinois. Once the respondents have participated in the preintervention surveys, the clinics will undergo technology training sessions to supplement implantation of technology at the clinic, and will be required to write up community health needs assessment reports on how the CHC is doing.

The reports will check progress of the community and provide feedback on where resources need to be allocated and what illnesses are most common, so that the CHCs can provide immunizations and preventive measures to the community.

Because the survey questions will vary among each respondent group, there will be different measurement for the two dependent variables: patient quality of care and cost effectiveness. For example, measurement of cost changes for a director may include percentage change in the clinic's patients who used the CHC over an ER/hospital, increased Medicaid reimbursement for the clinic's patients, and savings over time for the clinic's patients. The patient views cost in terms of expenses (amount spent per month) and savings over time. Physicians view cost as billable hours per month. The quality of care, similarly, will be measured for directors as improvements in efficiency and staff turnover, and patients will view care as improved services, quicker treatment, and quicker timeframe of receiving results as well as improved rate of medical errors. If the design is to show an impact by technology on the clinic's patients, there should be a statistically significant difference between preintervention period survey results and those that occur after the two-year period. All of the respondent groups must show a statistically significant positive increase in the added value to quality of care and cost effectiveness.

Patterns to be expected in segments of the population also will be identified through the course of the survey. For example, chronic care for African Americans at CHCs may increase in number, while more Hispanics will be treated for primary care. The statistical portion of the sample will be done using a multinomial logit function for each respondent group. The questions will target the needs, incentives, and concerns of each respondent group, so the measurement of improvements will differ. For example, the patient group will be asked how communication has changed between physician and patient. This same question may be asked of the physician as well, but measure of the communication will be whether or not the technology can translate and make up for language barriers that the paper records were not able to do previously. Next, the director will be asked about the language services and whether they are adequately available to the clinic's demographics. Major topics will be ascertained and then questions will be written on the perspective of the respondent group.

The major categories of survey questions will be changes in the CHCs, including:

1. Access to care
2. Communication between patients and physicians
3. Demographic changes for primary care
4. Changes in the incidence of primary care CHC attendance
5. Cost of care per unit (changes to cost per month, changes in Medicaid/Medicare settlements, etc.)
6. Precision—measured as prescription errors, medical errors, departmental errors
7. Coordination and staffing changes

A subject like coordination may not be as fitting for patients to answer, so a few basic questions may be asked about whether their results are transferred seamlessly across CHCs through the advancement of technological networks linking CHCs across a region. On the other hand, greater input will be provided by a director who has a thorough knowledge of the coordination networks between CHCs and other CHCs, between CHCs and hospitals, or CHCs and the emergency room. An example of access to care is an important issue, as well, that will be targeted for all the major respondent groups. This is important in the Midwest because cultural groups, such as Mormon populations across some counties, may receive more benefits from a clinic that can send outpatient care (staff from the clinic to the community) with mobile technology. Typically, these populations do not own cars and cannot commute to the clinics.

Next, looking at the open-ended portion of the survey, the responses may provide supplementation to the statistics portion of the survey. This way, a strictly quantitative survey that is based just on how numbers correlate and are controlled for the important variables truly fruitions into causation through a qualitative assessment and respondents who will report on their concerns without a necessary structure. This way, respondents can touch as well on any issues that were not provided through the questions portion of the survey. Some groups, especially disadvantaged groups, may see something that impacts them more positively or negatively, such as the issue of priority of their services. Some services may be a greater priority to disadvantaged groups, such as getting prescriptions for birth control, or mental or behavioral health needs, such as seeking a counselor for alcohol or drug abuse issues. These services are provided at community health center clinics, but may have long wait times. Whereas, the average patient may not see this as a need, patients of a very disadvantaged group may see wait times for services as an issue they can easily discuss in the focus group or observational study component of the survey more than the structured section.

This combination of the structured and open-ended format, as well as a breadth of various respondent groups, really provides a justification to outside researchers and the internal board on the project that this study is fortified and has coverage on all the major issues for the stakeholder groups of the issue. This is something that is new, innovative, and important during healthcare reform because studies that discuss all the stakeholders' perspectives in depth are rare. Validity issues that are bolstered in this study compared to a randomized experimental design are the external validity as the generalizability and reasonability of conducting such a survey is more probable. It is more difficult to conduct a study where patients are placed mandatorily in clinics. Here, the patients have freedom to continue attending the clinics of their choice, but are weighted and controlled for through statistics. At the same time, internal validity is not as strong as a completely random-ized study, but, by having groups of panel data as well as a longitudinal time frame and three survey respondent groups who all are linked to the CHCs in different ways, many of the major history, maturation, instrumentation, and validity issues of the survey are internally strengthened.

The final report for this component will be structured and organized with an abstract and summary of findings, a brief introduction to the study, measurement and survey design focus, written analysis of the project, and the final conclusion. However, weaved in, there will be charts and graphs to indi-cate the statistical comparisons across states, and present the findings with clarity of each respondent group. Conclusions will be drawn in three separate sections of findings from each respondent group and then analyzed together in order to see similarities, differences, and important revelations of their viewpoints on the effects of technology on the CHCs. Last, the appendix will provide the survey and a section will be attrib-uted to the respondents, with names and affiliations, so, if they were to be contacted for a follow-up in the future, there would be validity to the study.

## Conclusion

This chapter provides information about the state of com-munity health centers, and provides a sample research design that could be helpful to future projects on the state of HIT and CHCs. It identifies a variety of ways to analyze two major changes in CHCs: (1) the introduction of technology and technological effects into CHCs, and (2) the use of goal-setting and organizational behavior mechanisms, such as Community Health Needs Assessment (CHNA) reports that document inter-nal leadership and external county-level changes impacting CHCs. This study improvises on past research using both these components and conducting experiments that simultaneously analyze them. It also generates a combination of external and internal validity with the use of a survey research design and randomized experimental design. The patients identified are also from low-income and rural areas of the Midwest, which keeps the region fairly similar and less conducive to bias from geographic or other characteristics. The focus of the study is the time frame, to analyze a period during healthcare reform, which many studies have been unable to do since they were not done during a period of healthcare reform. This analysis is twofold, providing effects on patient quality of care and cost effectiveness, while also targeting specific patients, such as those who are uninsured and underinsured because changes to insurance coverage will be an important transition during health reform.

The policy analysis from this chapter is not just the outcomes research, such as the impact of health technology on CHCs and its impact on quality of care and cost, but also on the needs of diversified groups that can be studied. The subject of the chapter is very relevant during health reform because many papers so far have been unable to analyze the pre- and posthealth reform impacts on the uninsured groups and rurally underserved areas. However, more so than this, policy analysis can be gleaned from various subsets of the population and access to care. For example, differences in outcomes from CHCs can impact certain minority populations that have language barriers. This could be improved through technology usage. Other populations, such as African American with specific chronic conditions, may be more impacted by technology and CHNAs at CHCs because technology can prevent a lot of duplicated efforts that are expensive for chronic care treatment programs. Duplicated efforts can include multiple CAT scans, x-rays, and follow-up appointments as well as improved precision in the diagnosis of symptoms and problems. Another major target of CHCs is religious groups, such as Mormons, who have barriers to care including transportation and cultural limitations. They do not use normal forms of transportation (more so horses than cars), so it is difficult for them to frequently get treatment, thus, if one session with the doctor can prevent multiple follow-ups, it could tremendously increase utility of CHCs over the ER and other expensive programs.

More than just health disparities between groups and perceived wealth inequities is the issue of technological concerns itself. This research project shows the impacts of technology on health and where the money should be distributed within the organization's coffers, especially if certain supplements to technology, such as training programs, are most important for technology to take effect. Also, technological glitches may be revealed through this project that may be hindering progress for the outcomes of the study. Organizational behavior has become a fairly important topic, and it is closely linked to technological change, so it may be that both technological changes and goal setting through CHNAs are leading CHCs to be successful in their endeavors for the community. Organizational management of staff, through a more informed set of personnel may be important in keeping the clinic up to date on new additions to the technology as well as on changing laws, funding opportunities, and marketing techniques.

The other major policy implication from this project is how it integrates the community at the state, local, and federal level. Not only can one study how the community is being impacted, but also how funding for projects is limited by state and federal policies and investments, so this study has implications for the budget as well. How much investment there needs to be in Medicaid-eligible candidates, changes to the Medicaid requirements, and projections for the uninsured can supplement this study in providing better public policy analysis for society. This project has importance in the way that it points out improvements to preventative and primary care for those who need it most, and also will lessen the amount of taxpayer funding going toward paying for federal programs, if projected and conducted correctly. This is why this project has such scope and importance and should be considered seriously from a variety of fields and standpoints including public policy, economics, technology, organizational behavior, and healthcare research outcomes.

# References

Carroll, M., J. James, M. Lardiere, M. R. Proser, M. Sayre, J. Shore, and J. Temullo. 2010. Innovation networks for improving access and quality across the health care ecosystem. *Telemedicine and E-Health* 16, Jan.–Feb.: 107–111.

Chin, M., S. Auerbach, S. Cook, J. Harrison, J. Koppert, L. Jin, … and W. L. McNabb. 2000. Quality of diabetes care in community health centers. *American Journal of Public Health* 90, 431–434.

Chin, M., S. Cook, M. J. Drum, M. Guillen, C.A. Humikowski, J. Koppert, … and C. Schaefer. 2007. Improving diabetes care in Midwest community health centers with the health disparities collaborative. *Diabetes Care* 27, 2–8.

DeVoe, E. J., R. Gold, P. McIntire, J. Puro, S. Chauvie, and A. C. Gallia. 2011. Electronic health records vs Medicaid claims: Completeness of diabetes preventive care in community health centers. *Annals of Family Medicine* 9, July–Aug.: 351–359.

Gusmano, M. K., G. Fairbrother, and H. Park. 2002. Exploring the limits of the safety net: Community health centers and care for the uninsured. *Health Affairs* 21, 188–194, November/December.

Health Resources and Services Administration. 2006. *Comparison of the rural health clinic and federally qualified health center programs*. Washington, D.C.: U.S. Department of Health and Human Services, Office of Rural Health Policy.

Hicks, L. S. et al. 2006. The quality of chronic disease care at U.S. community health centers. *Health Affairs* 25, Nov./Dec.: 1712–1723.

Klein, D. J., A. B. Elster, D. Stevens, A. V. Hedberg, and A. R. Goodman. 2001. Improving adolescent preventive care in community health centers. *Pediatrics: Official Journal of the American Academy of Pediatrics* 107, February: 318–327.

Landon, B. E., L. S. Hicks, J. O'Malley, T. Lieu, T. Keegan, B. J. McNeil, and E. Guadagnoli. 2007. Improving the management of chronic disease care at community health centers. *The New England Journal of Medicine* 356, March: 921–934.

Lishner, D. M., and M. M. Richardson. 1996. *Access to primary health care among persons with disabilities in rural areas: A summary of the literature.* Rockville, MD: Agency for Healthcare Policy and Research.

McKinney, D., R. Kidney, C. Boselli, and A. Xu. 2010. *Entering the era of reform: The future of state funding for community health centers.* Washington, D.C.: State Policy Report, National Association of Community Health Centers.

Proser, M. 2005. Deserving the spotlight: health centers provide high-quality and cost-effective care. *Journal of Ambulatory Care Management* Oct.–Dec., 321–330.

Proser, M., J. E. Camacho, P. Edraos, and A. Stangis. 2011. Comparative performance of community health centers and other usual sources of primary care. (Commentary on Gurewich et al.) *Journal of Ambulatory Care Management* 34, 391–394.

Rothkopf, J., K. Brookler, S. Wadhwa, and M. Sajovetz. 2011. Medicaid patients seen at federally qualified health centers use hospital services less than those seen by private providers. *Health Affairs* 30, July: 1335–1342. Online at: http://www.cchn.org/pdf/health_centers/CCHN_HA_news_release.pdf

Shi, L., and A. D. Singh. 2004. *Delivering health care in America: A systems approach,* 4th ed. Burlington, MA: Jones & Barlett Publishers.

Shields, E. A., P. Shin, G. M. Leu, E. D. Levy, M. R. Betancourt, D. Hawkins, and M. Proser. 2007. Adoption of health information technology in community health centers: Results of a national survey. *Health Affairs* 26, 1373–1383.

# Chapter 7

# Small-Practice Physicians and HIT

## Chapter Summary

The purpose of this health information technology (HIT) study is to compare the adoption rates and factors affecting the adoption of electronic medical record (EMR) diffusion across two different geographical areas of small-practice-based physicians. The two examined areas were in the D.C./Virginia suburbs; one location was in the Fredericksburg region, and the other was in the D.C./VA metro region, commonly known as NOVA. Surveyors emailed or personally walked into small physician practices to conduct the Small Practice Study questionnaire, for physicians with or without EMRs. The survey was geared toward collecting information regarding the physicians' overall entrepreneurial experiences with EMRs and how they valued them for their small practices. EMR adoption rates and the general attitudes toward using EMRs were assessed in small-practice settings. Overall, we found that 10 different small physician practices scattered about the two regions were using EMRs throughout their entrepreneurial endeavors. Five practices in the out-skirts/Fredericksburg VA region and five practices in the D.C. metro/NOVA area had adopted an EMR system. Geography made a difference among the physicians' perceptions of the EMR's performance, however. Our first three hypotheses were supported by the evidence. Physicians in urban areas seem to be more interested in customer service quality standards, innovation, technology integration, and other entrepreneurial characteristics. They seemed more likely to implement technology, such as EMRs. Only the fourth hypothesis was inconclusive in its evidence as the relationship between EMRs and governmental incentives to adoption is unclear, if not lacking. Those in urban regions also were more likely to adopt than those in the outskirts, a sugges-tion that this trend may be based on entrepreneurial cultures across geographies.

## Why HIT? What Is It and How Can It Help Small-Practice Physicians?

An important U.S. healthcare policy issue is health information technology (HIT) adoption. This issue has grown in impor-tance in the past decade as many health organizations still have paper-based records when they could benefit from hav-ing and using electronic records. Electronic medical records, a fundamental component of HIT in health organizations, are said to improve efficiency and effectiveness by deriving higher quality of care while reducing costs. The government has pro-vided funding to healthcare organizations and health providers as incentives for HIT implementation, training, and projects. The American Recovery and Reinvestment Act (ARRA) and healthcare reform policies in the late 1990s and early 2000s have brought the issue of national HIT implementation into the forefront.

Some of the different purposes for HIT include creating an automated database of records, using electronic prescribing systems, ensuring data connectivity and coordination within and across organizations, and for tracking of large-scale national and international bioterrorism projects (Aetna Health, 2009). These purposes may be more useful to larger organizations than smaller ones, because of the large amount of data and need for a system to store and retrieve data in larger organizations. On the other hand, small practices may see more use in health technologies from communication benefits and customer relationship management than their larger organization peers, a theory being tested in this chapter. The development of an electronic network of connectivity makes HIT essential to all organizations so that real-time databases of health information can be developed and accessed by the globe.

The process of using health information technology has three stages: the actual adoption process (which involves access), implementation (at varying levels), and "meaningful use" (HIMSS, 2011). Successful use of HIT on a regular basis is considered meaningful use of HIT systems. The quantitative measurement of HIT implementation ranges from 0 to 7, with 7 considered meaningful use. This measurement technique was developed by the Healthcare Information Management Systems Society (HIMSS) to assess how far organizations are in their implementation process. The meaningful use stage has been achieved by only a small fraction of hospitals nationwide, and, for this reason, this chapter explores merely the presence or lack thereof of EMRs, rather than the stage of adoption.

HIT does come at a cost. The cost benefit analyses laid out by research has shown high short-run costs and potential long-run benefits, making it difficult for many organizations to envision the benefits that HIT can provide. Financial incentives have been provided by the government for hospitals that serve Medicare and Medicaid patients, because these hospitals typically have low reserves of capital and reimbursement policies to spend on large-scale technological infrastructure improvements. A survey by a market research firm, SK&A of Irvine, CA, found that nearly 21% of the surveyed participants weren't even aware that these meaningful use incentives existed. So, the overall speed of implementation has been slow and the interest in using the government incentives have been lacking. There is need for greater awareness of the long-run cost effectiveness and benefits to HIT and how it can be a solution to many of the current problems to improve the attitude toward HIT.

Health information technology has been adopted by different types of health organizations at varying speeds and with varying levels of interest. For for-profit hospitals, HIT implementation has been a smooth and fluid process. These organizations typically feel the need to be cutting edge in their research and quality of care. They also have the capital to adopt HIT. On the other hand, government hospitals have implemented and adopted technologies at a slower rate, possibly due to the size and ineffectiveness of the bureaucratic process. These hospitals have taken decades for even a few to adopt. Nonprofit hospitals, which are the majority (about 60%) of all hospitals, have wide variation in implementation, because some organizations have no knowledge of what electronic records are, while some organizations are meaningfully using the technology. In the case of small practices, with less than 10 employees, there seems to be evidence that adoption is extremely low. Findings from the Massachusetts survey proved that the practice size was strongly correlated with electronic health record (EHR) adoption (Simon et al., 2007). Of the total office practices that used EHRs, solo practices accounted for 14%; two to three physicians, 15%; four to six physicians, 33%; and seven plus physicians, 52% (a vast majority in the sampling) (Simon et al., 2007). Thus, small (fewer than three physicians) to medium-sized (four to six physicians) practices show a lower adoption rate as compared to larger seven plus physician-based offices (Simon et al., 2007).

## Physicians and Organizational Leadership

Collectively, the medical community's social systems that persuade adoption decisions view EHRs as a potential threat to professional autonomy (Ford et al., 2009). The physicians are apprehensive that policy makers, insurers, and administrators will manipulate EHRs as an alternative means to influence, restrict, or dictate how medicine will be practiced. Innovative physicians in small practices do not want to be micromanaged by these outside bureaucrats (Ford et al., 2009).

There are three educational solutions that the external shareholders can use to increase the internal social influence for small-practice physician EHR adoption. The first is medical education in the GME (graduate medical education) phase (Ford et al., 2009). The training of medical students to rely on EHRs and their decision support mechanisms can only boost the widespread EHR adoption rates. Secondly, the potential channel for internal persuasion in the social network of physicians is diluting the practice of EHRs with the continuing medical education (CME) requirement. They are solely dedicated to inform the physicians. Lastly, the prime social influence relates to that of academic detailing, which involved in-depth, one-on-one training sessions with physicians' behaviors and can forcefully impact their medical business norms (Ford et al., 2009).

A study was performed to measure the EHR adoption rates for all medical practices in the state of Massachusetts. Surveys were mailed to practices with different demographics (i.e., primary care versus specialty, hospital-affiliation, practice size, and rural versus urban) (Simon et al., 2007). It is representative for that of the rest of the U.S.'s medical practices.

Organizational factors play a crucial role in determining how rapidly EHRs will be adopted in the small-practice settings. Of such factors, the number of physicians in the practice and whether a practice is affiliated with a hospital system seem to drive the EHR adoption rates (Simon et al., 2007).

Small practices indicated the availability of incentives (i.e., governmental grants, regional health information organization funds, etc.) for adoption of HIT applications were more likely to use EHRs than those practices without incentives (33 versus 21%) (Simon et al., 2007). Furthermore, a trend from the study suggested that practices self-described as having innovative physicians were more likely to embrace EHRs (Simon et al., 2007).

From the Massachusetts survey, more than half of all respondents (59%) identified their own practice as an entrepreneurial organization that influenced the decision on whether to adopt a new EHR system. Practices that had not yet adopted EHRs disclosed that external organizations influenced the EHR adoption decision; however, fewer than one in five respondents overall suggested that the state medical society or specialty organizations played a role in the decision (Simon et al., 2007).

Technology adoption has been slow in the healthcare industry, and considerably more so for small practices and clinics, of less than 10 physicians. A study by SK&A Marketing Research found that only 30.8% of sole practitioner physician's offices had EMRs, compared to 63% of physician's offices with 6 to 10 physicians, and nearly 75.5% of organizations with 26 or more physicians. The gap in the adoption between small and large practices could be due to a number of reasons, for example, cultural, financial, socioeconomic, and more (Dolan, 2011). This chapter explores how the entrepreneurial capabilities—the administrative, clinical, customer service, and information technology aspects of doing business—impact a small-practice physician in his or her decision to adopt or not adopt EMR technology.

The presence of enterprise resource planning technologies has facilitated the use of EMRs and other HIT software in large hospitals, but smaller hospitals and practices have been left behind (Jenkins and Chistensen, 2001). Small practices generally do not have the capital to invest in such technologies, and may not see the need to invest due to cultural and socioeconomic reasons as well (Simon et al., 2007). The cultural aspects of this conundrum of why small practices are not able to adopt EMR technology is what is being explored in this chapter. The emphasis is on understanding what skills (entrepreneurial, communication, customer service oriented, etc.) may have an impact on adoption, based on the setting of the practice, which may differ by region, urban or rural locale, technological presence, and/or socioeconomic background of a region's population.

## Literature and Theories Relating to Technology Diffusion

Literature has discussed the importance of technology diffusion in various small and large organizations and the importance of customer service quality in healthcare organizations, but the literature does not marry these two ideas nor does it discuss the role of customer orientation and how it may influence technology adoption. The discussions in past research do not place emphasis on entrepreneurship and health providers' interest (or lack thereof) in their patient's satisfaction with the customer service and technology in a hospital. A possible hypothesis is that with greater interest in customer service quality and customer service orientation, there will be greater emphasis on technology adoption. Technology adoption should imply a benefit from an efficiency and effectiveness standpoint in healthcare, especially for a small practice. Two theories, technology diffusion theory and customer service quality, will lay the foundation for the importance of entrepreneurial spirit in adoption of HIT and may provide clarity for some of the results found.

## Technology Diffusion

The social components of technology diffusion, in particular EMR and EHR systems, play a significant role in consumers' decisions to adopt the systems rather than the economic or external factors (Ford et al., 2009). The internal influences on a provider's decision to adopt EHR technology, within their social network, are known as social contagions. It is this main social force that drives the adopter to acquire a new product technology. The physician's adoptions are an element of their exposure to other peer physicians' preexisting knowledge, attitudes, or behaviors concerning the new EHR technology (Ford et al., 2009).

In order to rapidly accelerate the EHR's technology diffusion within small-practice providers, the external constituents need to increase the social contagion effects that influence adoption decisions. Unless this occurs, the United States will consistently encounter low EHR adoption rates and delayed horizon times for adoption, by small practices (Ford et al., 2009).

## Customer Service and Quality

Parasuraman, Berry, and Zeithamil (1985) have highlighted the importance of analyzing service quality in an industry through various dimensions. Bitner et al. (2008) capture an important point in their work, which is that customer service is actually an experience that is shared through interactions between organizations, various processes, employees and customers, but also very much dependent on the customer's satisfaction, intent, and participation in a situation. In HIT usage, this is definitely the case, as low, medium, and high levels of participation are required in engaging health providers and ensuring they are implementing technology correctly. Hibbard et al. (2002) also discuss the two important roles patients play (co-producer and evaluator), which mean the participants are actively engaged in their care, and constantly evaluating care received, respectively. Kaplan (1989) discusses how the integration of the "patient–provider–information technology partnership" develops. Sullivan (2003) suggests the new patient-centered approach to medicine that has produced a different set of objectives for physicians and how they approach patients, which may at time seem subjective. The use of health IT in fostering objective outcomes of patient-centered characteristics, including comparisons of patients' health status and health behaviors may particularly impact small-practice physicians because their clientele (patients) may have an expectation from their local physician as to an understanding of cultural competency, language, similar values/beliefs, or tolerance to the patient. The physician may have an important decision to make when using health IT and incorporating it into their lifestyle, so that the physician does not lose their personal touch when bringing such objectivity (through IT) into practice.

The small-practice physician community does not have a convincing grasp of the quality improvement processes that are being targeted to them, by the adoption of EHR technology (Ford et al., 2009).

Small practices with EHRs were more likely to report that they were actively working to improve the quality of care. They also had formal email accounts, computerized scheduling systems, and e-prescribing applications (Simon et al., 2007).

## Barriers to Adoption

From the Massachusetts sample survey, on EHR adoption in office-based practices, a total of 1,884 physician practices were examined. More than 80% of the respondents identified that the start-up financial costs were a main concern for not implementing EHRs in the workplace (Simon et al., 2007). Additionally, from the study, reasons for barriers were further broken down into smaller categories and the overall top three choices for nonadoption were: (1) start-up financial costs (84%), (2) ongoing financial costs (82%), and (3) loss of productivity (81%).

Furthermore, the study discovered that a majority of physicians raised the technical factors in adoption as barriers. They included a lack of computer skills and knowledge, lack of technical support, lack of uniform standards, and the nonexistent technical interoperability for other clinical/administrative systems. Lastly, the bulk of physicians were worried about the privacy or security as a barrier to EHR technology adoption in their practices (Simon et al., 2007).

The Massachusetts EHR practice adoption level (23%) is more than double that of the national average (17.6%), and most of its physicians are regionally located in large group practices surrounding the urban area of Boston (Simon et al., 2007). Small practices maintain the vast majority of physicians who still have not tapped into the EHR. Massachusetts is a state that engages with widespread commerce technology and communications; however, the lack of pervasive EHR adoption in the market depicts the barriers facing physicians in small- and medium-sized practices throughout the country (Simon et al., 2007).

The presence of resource and routine rigidity may deter adoption. Christensen and Bowery (1996) describes resource rigidity as the lack of investment in "new resources necessary in a changing environment." On the other hand, *routine rigidity* discussed by Nelson and Winter (1982) is the inability to adapt and possibly improve organizational processes. These factors are characteristics of organizational inertia expanded on by Gilbert (2005), and can be applied to this piece. The likelihood of a technology investment in being disruptive may impact a practice's technology adoption status.

The more likely that the technology is disruptive, the more likely the practice will not adopt or integrate such technologies into its organizational infrastructure. Factors, such as external influences and adoption by peers, innovativeness and brand differentiation, and presence of a new opportunity, may lead to loosening of the routine rigidity and facilitate adoption.

## Looking to the Future: New Research

While the discussion of organizational culture in large health organizations is abundant, the research on small practices and their growth during health reform is still limited. The next section on health policy analyzes how small practices have been affected by change, their ability to cope with change, and their ability to cope with government regulation.

### *How Do Small Practices Deal with Change and Regulation?*

A small-business survey on the impacts of regulatory practices on small business by Harris Interactive and Accenture provides some input on the subject. The new healthcare bill is among the top three concerns for small businesses. Three examples of major problems envisioned by small physician practices from health reform include "growing regulatory and administrative burdens, rising malpractice costs, and declining reimbursements from insurers." Fewer doctors are projected to be self-employed, currently estimated at doctor self-employment rates of 33% (Accenture, 2011). New regulations, accountable care organization growth, and bureaucracy have driven away small private practices, and led to more hospitals swallowing up the small-timers.

Legislation on the topic also has been discussed. A political subcommittee was formed in July 2012, to discuss health reform and small private practices. Those who provided a statement and testimony included Merritt Hawkins & Associates; Louis F. McIntyre, M.D., Westchester Orthopedic Associates, White Plains Hospital Physicians, NY; Joseph M. Yasso, Jr, D.O., Heritage Physicians Group, Independence, MO; Jerry D. Kennett, M.D., F.A.C.C., senior partner, Missouri Cardiovascular Specialists, and vice president and chief medical officer of Boone Hospital Center in Columbia, MO.

Moving forward, it will be important to integrate the presence of healthcare reform and policies, efficient HIT adoption, and strong organizational culture to bring about a framework for physician practices to grow and succeed. The following three sections illustrate past behavior and predict future trends, while also providing analysis of how to improve the current state of healthcare in the United States.

## Methods

Using a survey provided to 10 small-practice physicians in the Northern Virginia (Alexandria, Arlington, Fairfax) and suburban Virginia (Fredericksburg) areas, survey results were collected regarding the entrepreneurial capabilities and cultural factors likely to impact physicians to adopt technology. Then, the survey results were interpreted to gauge how these factors played a role in EMR adoption at the practices.

The major focus areas of the survey were customer service quality and EMR adoption. Customer service quality had to do with the perceptions of physicians and the efficiency, reliability, and other features that may come out of using EMRs. The dependent variable of the study is the adoption or lack thereof of EMRs, and the independent variables included: fear toward technology (technological inertia), customer service orientation, resource and routine rigidity, and government and other financial barriers. Next, the author presents hypotheses for the study before introducing the methodology used to conduct the surveys.

## Hypotheses

**Hypothesis 1:** Doctors in metro areas will have higher customer service quality standards and will be more likely to implement technology.

**Hypothesis 2:** Doctors with more entrepreneurial qualities have a higher likelihood of implementing EMRs.

**Hypothesis 3:** Doctors who perceive technology as a threat will not adopt.

**Hypothesis 4:** Knowledge of government incentives is more likely to impact the adoption of EMRs for those with customer-oriented (entrepreneurial) abilities, more so than those who do not place focus on a customer orientation.

## Survey Findings

First, overall findings are provided in Table 7.1 to suggest how small practices in each region compared, across various technological and organizational characteristics. As can be seen from Table 7.1, the responses to survey questions showed that Metro area small practices seemed to have greater emphasis on customer service quality, EMR adoption, and innovation.

As can be seen from Table 7.1, the responses to survey questions showed that Metro area small practices seemed to have greater emphasis on customer service quality, EMR adoption, and innovation. On the other hand, many of the government incentives in EMR adoption (both positive and negative) seem to impact the small practices in Metro areas more, especially because penalties affect the small practices in Metro areas.

Demographics are presented in Table 7.2.

**Table 7.1  Perceptions of EMRs as Beneficial**

| | *Overall: Who Perceived Better Results?* | |
|---|---|---|
| *Characteristic* | *Outskirts/ Fredericksburg/ Leesburg area* | *Metro Area/NOVA* |
| EMRs usefulness | | X |
| EMR quality of care | | X |
| EMR vendor rating | | X |
| Routine rigidity | X | |
| Gov. financial incentives | About the same, both gov. benefits and penalties perceived more for NOVA | |
| HIEs' usefulness | X | |
| Small-practice flexibility/ innovation | | X |

As can be seen, more specialists answered the survey in the Metro area region, which may be why the Metro area perceived EMRs as beneficial. Specialists may see more use out of EMR functioning. Only one urgent care clinic answered the survey in the suburban regions, compared to none in the NOVA region, and no walk-in clinics or concierge practices. The majority of the survey was primary and specialty care, with an emphasis on single specialty.

The following tables include many of the specific survey questions broken down individually.

In Table 7.3, we found that all of the physicians "Agreed" or "Strongly Agreed" that EMR usage/functioning were beneficial for their quality of care to the patients. The Metro area is more likely to "Strongly Agree" about the quality of care being valuable using EMRs.

In Table 7.4, we found that all but one of the physicians "Agreed" or "Strongly Agreed" that EMRs would be helpful for tracking their patients' care. One doctor in the Outskirts/VA

**Table 7.2 Demographics**

| | Outskirts/ Fredericksburg/VA | Metro Area & NOVA |
|---|---|---|
| **Founder** | 5 | 5 |
| Nonfounder | 0 | 0 |
| **Type of Specialist** | | |
| Primary care | 4 | 3 |
| Specialty care | 1 | 2 |
| Urgent care | 1 | 0 |
| Walk-in clinic | 0 | 0 |
| Concierge practice | 0 | 0 |
| **Single or Multispecialty?** | | |
| Single specialty | 5 | 3 |
| Multispecialty | 0 | 2 |
| **Number of full-time equivalent (FTE) physicians** | | |
| 1 | 0 | 1 |
| 2 | 1 | 1 |
| 3 to 5 | 3 | 2 |
| 6 to 10 | 1 | 1 |
| 11 or more | 0 | 0 |
| Customer service quality | | X |
| EMR/PHR use & integration | | X |

geographic region found EMRs as "Neutral." Small practices in NOVA seem to think EMRs are more useful than offices in the outskirts.

As seen in Table 7.5, physicians in the outskirts may rely on word of mouth more in their selection of EMRs. They had more interactions with other peers about EMR selection than

**Table 7.3   EMRS Are Beneficial to Quality of Care**

| EMRs Are Beneficial, as They Will Improve the Quality of Care | | |
|---|---|---|
| Answer | Outskirts/VA | Metro Area & NOVA |
| Strongly Disagree (1) | 0 | 0 |
| Disagree (2) | 0 | 0 |
| Neutral (3) | 0 | 0 |
| Agree (4) | 4 | 3 |
| Strongly Agree (5) | 1 | 2 |

that of the Metro/NOVA-area physicians. The Metro/NOVA practices had communicated via online forums as a means to differentiate the types of EMRs. The Outskirts/Fredericksburg did not use that tool for adoption promotion.

PHRs seem to be more useful to those in the NOVA region, possibly because there is greater integration between PHRs and EHRs in NOVA (Table 7.6). The Outskirts region was somewhat neutral regarding the interoperability aspect of EHRs and PHRs.

## Vendors

Physicians in the Outskirts region did not have answers to questions on the vendors, and did not regard their service

**Table 7.4   EMRs Are Beneficial for Patients**

| Answer | Outskirts/VA | Metro Area & NOVA |
|---|---|---|
| Strongly Disagree (1) | 0 | 0 |
| Disagree (2) | 0 | 0 |
| Neutral (3) | 1 | 0 |
| Agree (4) | 3 | 4 |
| Strongly Agree (5) | 1 | 1 |

**Table 7.5 Interaction During EMR Selection**

| Did You Get a Chance to Interact with Other Physicians or Fellow Small-Practice Owners during the Time of EMR Selection? | | |
|---|---|---|
| *Answer* | *Outskirts* | *Metro Area/NOVA* |
| Yes | 4 | 2 |
| No | 0 | 3 |
| Sometimes | 1 | 0 |
| Do You Participate in Any Online Forums That Focus on the Types of EMRs or the Benefits of Each Type of EMR for Your Practice? | | |
| *Answer* | *Outskirts* | *Metro Area/NOVA* |
| Yes | 0 | 3 |
| No | 4 | 2 |
| Sometimes | 1 | 0 |

highly. This may be due to the fact that their implementation is still ongoing and/or the vendors have completed their contractual agreements by maintaining customer support for a certain period of time since the EMRs go-live date (Table 7.7 and Table 7.8).

**Table 7.6 Selection of EMRs**

| Small-to-Medium Practices Should Select EMRs That Would Include Patient Portals and PHRs That Allow Patients to View Their Records, Lab Results, etc. | | |
|---|---|---|
| *Answer* | *Outskirts* | *Metro Area/NOVA* |
| Strongly Agree (1) | 0 | 0 |
| Agree (2) | 2 | 4 |
| Neutral (3) | 2 | 1 |
| Disagree (4) | 1 | 0 |
| Strongly Disagree (5) | 0 | 0 |
| No Answer (6) | 0 | 0 |

**Table 7.7  Vendors**

| Vendors Have Prompt Customer Service and All I Need Is to Call Them to Get Any Help | | |
|---|---|---|
| Answer | Outskirts | Metro Area/NOVA |
| Strongly Disagree (1) | 0 | 0 |
| Disagree (2) | 2 | 0 |
| Neutral (3) | 2 | 0 |
| Agree (4) | 1 | 2 |
| Strongly Agree (5) | 0 | 3 |
| No Answer (6) | 0 | 0 |
| No Answer | 0 | 0 |
| *Ongoing Support from Vendors* | | |
| Answer | Outskirts | Metro Area/NOVA |
| Strongly Disagree (1) | 0 | 0 |
| Disagree (2) | 0 | 0 |
| Neutral (3) | 3 | 0 |
| Agree (4) | 0 | 2 |
| Strongly Agree (5) | 0 | 3 |
| No Answer (6) | 2 | 0 |

## Government Impacts on EMR Usage

Small practices in NOVA were more motivated by government incentives to use EMRs (Table 7.8). While both regions agree on government penalties being a big reason for switching over to an EMR, it will impact NOVA offices more than the Outskirts/VA offices.

## Routine Rigidity

None of the Metro area practices found that EMR adoption would be disruptive to their ongoing routines of providing

**Table 7.8   Government Incentives**

| Government Incentives Motivated Me to Use an EMR | | |
|---|---|---|
| *Answer* | *Outskirts/VA* | *Metro Area & NOVA* |
| Strongly Disagree (1) | 1 | 2 |
| Disagree (2) | 0 | 0 |
| Neutral (3) | 2 | 0 |
| Agree (4) | 2 | 0 |
| Strongly Agree (5) | 0 | 3 |
| The Government Is after Me to Get This Done or Otherwise I Will Be Facing Penalties | | |
| *Answer* | *Outskirts/VA* | *Metro Area & NOVA* |
| Strongly Disagree (1) | 0 | 0 |
| Disagree (2) | 1 | 0 |
| Neutral (3) | 0 | 0 |
| Agree (4) | 1 | 0 |
| Strongly Agree (5) | 3 | 5 |

patient care with the EMRs (Table 7.9). The Outskirts, however, found that it may create a bottleneck with the normal work-flows of care in their practices.

NOVA doctors thought health information exchanges (HIEs) were less useful as compared to the Outskirts physicians (Table 7.10). Having innovative technology and reaching patients to produce a standard of customer service quality were characteristics more likely to be found in metro area practices (Table 7.11).

The importance of innovation is represented by NOVA, more so than the regions that are outskirts to the city. Trending from Table 7.12, the NOVA physicians value the piece on allocating more resources toward financing a new innovation, such as EMRs, as compared to the Outskirts practices.

**Table 7.9    Routine Rigidity**

| *Small-to-Medium Practices Have to Follow Certain Routines of Providing Patient Care and They Cannot Change That Easily* | | |
|---|---|---|
| *Answer* | *Outskirts* | *Metro Area/NOVA* |
| Strongly Disagree (1) | 0 | 2 |
| Disagree (2) | 3 | 3 |
| Neutral (3) | 0 | 0 |
| Agree (4) | 2 | 0 |
| Strongly Agree (5) | 0 | 0 |

**Table 7.10    Usefulness of Health Information Exchanges**

| *Do You Think the Health Information Exchanges (HIEs) Are Useful?* | | |
|---|---|---|
| *Answer* | *Outskirts* | *Metro Area/NOVA* |
| Very useful and informative | 1 | 1 |
| Somewhat useful | 2 | 2 |
| Neutral | 2 | 0 |
| Not useful | 0 | 2 |
| Not at all useful or informative | 0 | 0 |
| Other | 1 | 0 |

## Results and Analysis

Based on these results, we found that all the hypotheses for the chapter were correct except about some of the government incentives as well as the functioning of the HIEs. The first hypothesis about doctors in Metro areas having higher customer service quality standards and will be more likely to implement technology was true, because impacts from routine rigidity were less for these doctors, and they seemed to be the most innovative and technology accepting. The second hypothesis about doctors with more entrepreneurial qualities

**Table 7.11   Customer Service Quality**

| *I Am a Tech-Savvy Person and I Have Always Tried to Get the Best Technology Available for My Practice* | | |
|---|---|---|
| *Answer* | *Outskirts/VA* | *Metro Area/NOVA* |
| Strongly Disagree (1) | 0 | 1 |
| Disagree (2) | 2 | 1 |
| Neutral (3) | 1 | 0 |
| Agree (4) | 1 | 1 |
| Strongly Agree (5) | 1 | 2 |
| *Small-to-Medium Practices Should Be Constantly in Touch with Patients and Get Their Feedback* | | |
| *Answer* | *Outskirts* | *Metro Area/NOVA* |
| Strongly Agree (1) | 0 | 3 |
| Agree (2) | 2 | 2 |
| Neutral (3) | 2 | 0 |
| Disagree (4) | 1 | 0 |
| Strongly Disagree (5) | 0 | 0 |

**Table 7.12   Importance of Innovation**

| *When Small-to-Medium Practices Allocate Resources: It Is Highly Recommended That They Allocate a Substantial Amount for New Innovations* | | |
|---|---|---|
| *Answer* | *Outskirts* | *Metro Area/NOVA* |
| Strongly Agree (1) | 1 | 2 |
| Agree (2) | 0 | 3 |
| Neutral (3) | 2 | 0 |
| Disagree (4) | 2 | 0 |
| Strongly Disagree (5) | 0 | 0 |
| No Answer | 0 | 0 |

being more likely to implement technology was harder to show correlations from this study, so we cannot draw any firm conclusions from the survey results to this hypothesis. The third hypothesis about doctors who perceive technology as a threat, so they will not adopt, was true, because many of the suburban practices showed technology averse characteristics and, therefore, were less likely to adopt EMRs or to think EMRs were beneficial to their patients.

Finally, the fourth hypothesis about knowledge of government incentives being impactful on the adoption of EMRs for those with customer-oriented (entrepreneurial) abilities, more so than those who do not place focus on a customer orientation, seemed true, except that this was more due to the power of government penalties that seemed a bigger concern for the NOVA region small practices. Government-run HIEs, on the other hand, were less impactful, because many of the NOVA-region small practices did not see them as useful, whereas the suburban region practices did. This could mean that some of the EMR-related efforts may impact certain small practices more than others, based on entrepreneurial ability, customer service orientation, knowledge of government incentives, and more. It also may be a lesson to the fact that marketing has to cater to all kinds of EMR users to be effective.

One of the limitations of the study was the small sample size. If the study could be done on a larger population, the results could be representative of the population. For now, the study provides an example for further research.

## Conclusion and Recommendations

In conclusion to the findings from the EMR survey, we were able to find evidence to support our first three hypotheses. The first hypothesis held true to the fact that urban area physicians have higher customer service quality standards and will be more likely to implement technology such as EMRs. The second hypothesis had enough valid evidence revealing that doctors with more entrepreneurial qualities will have a higher likelihood of implementing EMRs. Based on the innovation characteristic, focus on customer service quality, greater interest in vendor characteristics, and integration with multiple technology systems (such as PHRs), we could consider the organizations with these characteristics to be more entrepreneurial in nature. Our third hypothesis was confirmed to be true, about how doctors who perceive technology as a threat will not adopt. The suburban physicians showed a stronger concern with an EMR implementation. Finally, the fourth hypothesis was inconclusive in its evidence as the relationship between EMRs and governmental incentives to adoption is unclear, if not lacking. Overall, the evidence suggests that physicians that possess greater entrepreneurial abilities and have more customer orientation to their patients will tend to adopt the EMR application faster than those who are less customer-oriented. This was especially true for those in urban regions. As an overall rating, the author would state that those healthcare organizations in urban areas are better suited to technology adoption, possibly due to factors, such as customer orientation and geographical traits, which improve potential for EMR implementation.

Geography may have played a role in possible differences among entrepreneurs. This could be the reason for other studies on how geography has an effect on HIT adoption and diffusion across different regions. Those in the outskirts believed in more community-based, word-of-mouth communication, with an emphasis on HIEs. They perceived the HIEs as a way to alleviate information asymmetry. They also perceived that routine rigidity was one of the greatest hindrances to HIT. They found that having to make an effort beyond the normal routine was cumbersome.

Some of these geographical factors may impact cultural setting as well. The customer orientation of those in suburban regions may have been focused on word-of-mouth and community-based entrepreneurship over the urban characteristics of emailing customers or using electronic means to communicate with patients. This is an important factor to note, and gives way to suggestions for future studies. Analyzing what these cultural factors are that may differ between suburban and urban regions and how these play a role in physician entrepreneurship, as well as service quality perceptions, will better suggest how EMRs are perceived and whether they will be valued more as suburban regions increase usage of technology. This recommendation is heavily based on Rogers (2003), who perceived technology diffusion as contingent on cultural factors and "observability" in a community, just as much as other factors, such as cost, economics, and perceived benefits. The observability of usefulness the EMR has in NOVA versus in Frederickburg may have impacted the integration of the EMR in the small-practice setting in each place.

On the other hand, HIT was perceived as useful, a source of innovation, a source of improvement of customer service, and as causing improvements to quality of care standards primarily for those small practices in NOVA. The NOVA organizations were more likely to have EMR and PHR integration methods as well. This seems quite intuitive as these organizations may have more interaction with large urban hospitals that are also technology intensive. Another one of the factors Rogers (2003) suggested as impacting technology adoption was the relative advantage, or how useful an innovation is perceived to be over others. EMRs seemed to be a relative advantage to NOVA over the Fredericksburg region.

Interestingly, neither organization perceived government financial incentives as being effective. This is one of the major areas for improvement, and could have important policy consequences. Governments need to focus on the aspect of improving communication with their small practices in order to address this and describe how these organizations will be affected by the HITECH act, EMR adoption, and more. This could change how small practices perceive the financial, social, and ethical implications of EMR usage.

# References

Accenture. (2011, August). Adapting to a new model of physician employment. Retrieved from  HYPERLINK "http://www.accenture.com/SiteCollectionDocuments/PDF/Accenture-Outlook-Physician-Trends-August-2011-No2.pdf" http://www.accenture.com/SiteCollectionDocuments/PDF/Accenture-Outlook-Physician-Trends-August-2011-No2.pdf

Aetna Health. 2009. A summary of the HITECH Act. Online at: http://www.athenahealth.com/_doc/pdf/HITECH_Fact_Sheet_Whitepaper.pdf (accessed June 2012).

Bitner, M., A. L. Ostrom, and F. N. Morgan. 2008. Service blueprinting: A practical technique for service innovation. *California Management Review* 50 (3): 66–94.

Dolan, P. L. 2011. Why small medical practices lag in EMR adoption. Online at: http://www.amednews.com/article/20111107/business/311079967/2/

Ford, E. W., N. Menachemi, L. T. Peterson, and T. R. Huerta. 2009. Resistance is futile: But it is slowing the pace of EHR adoption nonetheless. *Journal of American Medical Informatics Association* 16, 274–281.

Gilbert, C. 2005. Unbundling the structure of inertia: Resource versus routine rigidity. *Academy of Management Journal* 48 (5): 741–763.

Healthcare Information and Management Systems Society (HIMSS). 2011. The positive impact of health IT to improve care of patients with diabetes, Chicago.

Hibbard, J. H., P. Slovic, E. M. Peters, et al. 2002. Strategies for reporting health plan performance information to consumers: Evidence from controlled studies. *Health Service Research Journal* 37, 291–313.

Nelson, R. R., and S. G. Winter. 1982. *An evolutionary theory of economic change.* Cambridge MA: Harvard University Press.

Parasuraman, A., L. L. Berry, and V. A. Zeithaml. 1985. A conceptual model of service quality and its implications for future research. *Journal of Marketing* 49 (4): 41–50.

Rogers, E. M. 2003. *Diffusion of innovations. Elements of Diffusion,* 5th ed. New York, NY: The Free Press, pp. 1–38.

Simon, S. R., R. Kaushal, P. D. Cleary, C. A. Jenter, L. A. Volk, E. G. Poon, E. J. Orav, H. G. Lo, D. H. Williams, and D. W. Bates. 2007. Correlates of electronic health record adoption in office practices: A statewide survey. *Journal of American Medical Informatics Association* 14, 110–117.

# Chapter 8

# The Micro, Meso, and Macro Perspectives of HIT Adoption

## Chapter Summary

The introduction of health information technology (HIT) has focused on the objectives of increased accessibility, quality of care, and increased privacy and security, to name a few. This chapter will document issues, challenges, and interests posed by using HIT, specifically quality of care and privacy considerations, and its consequences on big data. The issues are grouped at the macro, meso, and micro-levels of policies in big data, to better represent the categories of problems faced in the big data world, and policy solutions for these problems. The macro-level considerations discuss the research question of the impact of the U.S. government's Health Insurance Portability and Accountability Act (HIPAA) on the violation of big data concerns, using two hypotheses. The first hypothesis predicts that the introduction of HIPAA standards will increase deidentification of data, but may increase cyber security concerns and risks for health and computer industries. The meso-level research question discusses the impact of organizational level changes on big data concerns. The first hypothesis predicts intraorganizational standards and changes that will improve HIPAA compliance, the second hypothesis predicts that organizational redesign and implementation of the patient-centered medical homecare (PCMH) model will improve big data risks, and the third hypothesis predicts that the presence of the cloud may have varying impacts on big data, quality of care, and privacy of health information. The micro-level research question analyzes consumers' involvement in their own healthcare, through social media and personal health record portals, and how it creates increased health awareness and interest in health information, while posing challenges to big data security and privacy. The micro-level hypothesis predicts that an increase in consumer involvement in health information may impact big data negatively, though the second hypothesis suggests that informed consent may improve the state of big data if more individuals are knowledgeable about the usage of health information on the Web.

## Introduction

The direction that the electronic health industry is moving toward is a completely electronic state of health records and health information across the nation, as suggested by legislation relating to the Health Information Technology for Economic and Clinical Health (HITECH) Act and the Patient Protection and Affordable Care Act (PPACA), the U.S.'s new health reform law. In the event that the nation becomes fully electronic, there will be repercussions on the quality of health services, consumer health technologies, and privacy and security issues of big data. This chapter will document issues, challenges, and interests posed by big data and health information exchanges across big data portals. The issues are grouped at the macro, meso, and micro levels of policies in big data, to better represent the categories of problems faced in the big data world, and policy solutions for these problems. The macro-level considerations include the impact of the U.S. government's HIPAA on the violation of big data concerns for consumers through deidentification of data and the impact on cyber security risks for health and computer industries. The meso-level research question includes intraorganizational changes, such as organizational redesign, implementation of the PCMH model, and the presence of the cloud, which impacts big data, quality of care, and privacy of health information. The micro-level research question analyzes consumers' involvement in their own healthcare, through social media and personal health record portals, and how it creates increased health awareness and interest in health information, while posing challenges to big data security and privacy. First discussed are the macro-level challenges from the government privacy policy that impacts big data and quality of care.

## Macro-Level Policies and Considerations

The macro-level policies of big data involve the government and the consumers, organizations, and vendors that abide by the privacy, security, and policy guidelines on big data. The overarching policy in the realm of big data is HIPAA, which documents the guidelines and relationships between organizations, individuals, and the exchange of health information. By analyzing the macro-level research question of what impacts does HIPAA have on quality of care for consumers and government data security, the author analyzed two hypotheses. The first looks at the implications of HIPAA on deidentification of data and data security for consumers. The second analyzes the consequences of HIPAA on cyber security for organizations and the nation as a whole.

> **Research Question:** What impacts does HIPAA have on quality of care for consumers and government data security?

> **Hypothesis 1**: Deidentification of big data may be improved by complying with, and building trust, on HIPAA. Deidentification of big data may result in increased health research.

The first research question analyzes how government efforts through HIPAA impact deidentification of big data. Deidentified data is a method of concealing personal information linked to individuals, such that the data no longer can be used to identify an individual and his or her health information. The purpose of deidentified data is that it is safer to store and exchange data between organizations and governments if it is not linked to individuals and can be used then for market and scientific research. The hypothesis that HIPAA standards may strengthen individual trust in one's health information can be supported by work from McGraw (2012). McGraw analyzed the implications of deidentifying big data using HIPAA standards, which involve deletion of about 18 variables that may closely identify personal health information, including a patient's name and address. One of the benefits of using HIPAA standards for deidentifying big data is that, in postdeidentification, the data is no longer HIPAA regulated and can be used for research purposes. Yet, challenges found from using HIPAA compliance include the knowledge that no deidentified data can be at a "zero risk" level, and that the deidentified data may not propose as much benefit for health services research due to lack of geographic and other demographic and health-specific information (McGraw et al., 2012). To provide for research with some restricted, identifiable information, there are also "limited datasets," but they are closely restricted for usage in research. The use of deidentified big data may be affected by presence of consumer information that is anonymously posted on the Internet, but which may be used to identify consumers with the big data (McGraw et al., 2009). This poses a challenge because information may be deidentified using a rigorous HIPAA methodology, but individual posting of information on the Web may make identification easier, a problem known as "easy reidentification results." Yet, data suggests that HIPAA standards for deidentification have resulted in a very low reidentification rate of 0.013% (El Emam et al., 2011). The consumer involvement in reidentification of their health information will be discussed in greater detail in the Micro-Level Challenges section below.

Some of the benefits of HIPAA standards of deidentification are the rigorous and robust methodologies used, and security safeguards present against reidentification. Trust in these standards is important, though difficult to achieve. A combination of consumer compliance in keeping data deidentified and transparency in the use and ethics of deidentified big data is especially important. For example, the U.S.'s new health reform law, the PPACA, poses new restriction on health insurance companies so that they cannot use pre-existing conditions to cherry pick the healthier patients into their insurance plans. Similarly, the use of big data must be transparent and guided by ethical purposes in research, and not be used to hurt the consumer, especially when exchanged between organizations. The fear is that organizations will unfairly use big data to their advantage in selecting patients and trying to reap the greatest profits. Developing this level of trust, as suggested by McGraw (2012) will create an environment of HIPAA compliance and acceptance to deidentified big data by organizations and consumers.

The analysis provides support for the fact that HIPAA compliance in deidentifying data can produce a smooth transition and benefit for big data research and by protecting the personal health information of consumers. The next hypothesis analyzes HIPAA impacts on cyber security, and suggests reasons to uphold the impact of macro (governmental) policies.

**Hypothesis 2**: HIPAA compliance may increase the need for cyber security across health and health-related industries.

HIPAA was first introduced in 1996, when various other electronics, such as computer systems and the Internet, were being used in many major industries in the United States. Because HIPAA impacts vendors, healthcare businesses, health organizations, and even organizations that are on business agreements with healthcare organizations, HIPAA guidelines have greatly impacted the computer security industry as a whole, as discussed by Mercuri (2004). The original guidelines of HIPAA were "health insurance reform" and "administrative simplification," which now carry over to even nonhealth-related businesses that may be working on health information, patients, and a wide variety of stakeholders. The presence of globalization and the computer industry that now connects big data across large geographic regions can mean that the entire cyber security industry can be at risk when sharing big data. For this reason, HIPAA standards provide a way to mitigate the risks of sharing big data across industries. There are HIPAA compliant regulations, such as ISO (International Organization of Standardization) Common Criteria (CC), which provide security for defense-related projects and has been noted for strength in equipment design, construction, and recordkeeping. The computer industry has found ways to meet HIPAA compliance and also produce stronger security for cyber threats, using the CC status. For example, Persona 5.0 is a program (produced by a French company called Esker), which is "compliant with certain U.S. Department of Defense policies, as well as the Internet security policy requirements of the U.S. Health Care Financing Administration" (Mercuri, 2004). Other examples include Alacris, Inc., which uses CC certification for pharmaceutical and health products, financial services, and government clients. The presence of HIPAA-compatible products that have many purposes produces flexibility for organizations that have health and nonhealth-related services, and require multifaceted computer systems with different kinds of security. Though these examples provide hope in HIPAA guidelines, Mercuri discusses the problems for most organizations in HIPAA compliance, related to high costs for training resources and staff, and time to shift into the new procedures. HIPAA takes the "full involvement" of a group of health staff, and may not be as easy as certification would seem. HIPAA administration requires meso-level, organizational safeguards, including "policy and procedures development, incident response and recovery, evaluation of business associate contracts, hiring and termination impacts, compliance and awareness training," which are discussed next. At a macro level, HIPAA violations may occur due to the complexity of advanced technological health data, including lab results, CAT scans, x-rays, and much more, which are exchanged on a regular basis between government and nongovernmental entities (Mercuri, 2004). Internet viruses and deletion and corruption of data also pose threats to secure health information at the big data level, especially for industries that use high-level computer systems and technical data. There is still not enough safeguards of big data across the industry level to ensure that information is stored and transferred in a safe manner, and can be secure from all risks of cyber attacks.

Challenges have been found in sharing big data across industries because of unknown boundaries in what data is safe to exchange and whether or not it is fully HIPAA compliant. Examples of major breaches in HIPAA compliance leading to increased security threats in the health industry include the example of a hospital (name left anonymous by Health and Human Services (HHS)) that treated a patient for a sports injury, and then released information to the local media, featuring sensitive information, including the x-ray of the patient. The hospital was required to develop new disclosure policies before providing such data again to any third-party source (HHS, 2012). Another example was a pharmacy chain that made personal identified health information accessible to all patients at the over-the-counter service, leading to a breach in the pharmacy's HIPAA policies, and violations in the pharmacy chain in turning over HIPAA-compliant information to a law enforcement agency (HHS, 2012). The pharmacy chain was required to revise its national policies on information disclosure to comply with HIPAA and protect health information, while also complying with national and state laws. Such examples suggest the serious concern that HIPAA standards may pose to the health industry at the macro level and the careful balance between HIPAA guidelines, organizational- and industry-level guidelines, and national and state laws that must be in compliance. Because big data is used by many third parties beyond healthcare organizations, it becomes less transparent as to what data can be shared and whether the exchange meets HIPAA compliance standards. For this reason, mistakes from the first few years of HIPAA compliance are providing support for new policies to ensure safer transactions of big data.

At the macro level, HIPAA policies enforced by the U.S. government are impacting the deidentification of data and the storage and transfer of data across the industry. HIPAA standards play an important role, though these standards pose challenges for organizations that must engage in transactions with nonhealth organizations and nonhealth data. HIPAA may help protect against cyber security threats, though there is a need for increased security and procedures to safeguard health data, even if the data is HIPAA compliant. Next, the author analyzes a meso-level perspective of organizational policies that produce big data concerns when trying to improve health quality, consumer centric objectives, and privacy concerns.

# Meso-Level Challenges to Electronic Medical Record (EMR) Adoption

To depict a particular case of the problems with big data at the meso, or organizational level, the author provides the example of Rite Aid. Rite Aid chains were found to be incorrectly disposing of prescriptions and labeled pill bottles with individuals' identifiable information in trash containers, making the pills easily obtainable by the public. This HIPAA violation led to a lawsuit and $1 million settlement for Rite Aid. The company has had to develop new policies to assure the HIPAA compliance of its patients' health information. The example of numerous organizations, such as Rite Aid, that have faltered in providing strong, internal organizational policies that comply with HIPAA and produce risks to privacy and security of big data suggests a critical need for changes in the organizational implementation of HIPAA. The meso-level research question asks: What kinds of organizational policies and strategies are required to ensure increased privacy and security of big data within and across health organizations? Three hypotheses suggest how organizations may be able to work toward strategies for improved privacy and security of their big data while also working toward patient-centered outcomes and quality care.

**Research question:** What kinds of organizational policies and strategies are required to ensure increased privacy and security of big data within and across health organizations?

**Hypothesis 1:** Intraorganizational commitment to fulfilling HIPAA compliance will increase privacy and security for organizations and their big data storage and exchange.

Specific characteristics in health organizations and organizations handling health data seem to be associated with increased standards of privacy and security for the organizations' big data as well as HIPAA compliance. Some of these organizational characteristics include incorporating HIPAA compliance in the subcultures of organizational staff, culture of the organizations' security practices, and producing balance between formal and informal guidelines and objectives (Collmann and Cooper, 2007; Kwon and Johnson, 2013). To depict how organizational commitment can lead to HIPAA compliance, the author has provided a few examples. Collmann and Cooper analyze the characteristics that led to a security breach of Kaiser Permanente's Internet Patient Portal. They found that the nature of the information system potentially can affect the organization's ability to respond to a crisis, because complex computer systems can cause greater crisis and difficulties in mitigating problems. Security training within the organization provided help in the breach incident, but could not stop other information security breaches, even though the information was HIPAA compliant. Reform and transition periods require a good deal of emphasis from all organizational staff, and are not limited to information technology (IT) personnel, as also suggested by Kwon and Johnson. The example of the Kaiser information security breach suggests that HIPAA may not stop an information security breach, but it may help protect and reduce the consequences of such a breach. It also suggests that, at a subcultural level, HIPAA compliance should be of importance to all staff.

Similarly, Kwon and Johnson (2013) compare the type of security standards and HIPAA/HITECH security objectives met by various organizations to analyze organizational culture characteristics. They find that there are three major clusters of organizations that meet security standards: leaders, followers, and laggers. It was found that a balance between technical and nontechnical practices was associated with the highest security standards, which suggest the need for informal and formal practices to guide HIPAA compliance. Kwon and Johnson found that the need for "ensuring third parties' breach management and training" was most important for organizations that wanted to produce the highest level of compliance to security and privacy standards. Organizational characteristics, such as strong training across subcultures and all personnel as well as training for crisis management and HIPAA compliant security objectives, produce the most beneficial meso-level strategies for usage of big data. The next hypothesis analyzes the PCMH as a potential framework that can support improved big data standards at the organizational level.

**Hypothesis 2:** Development of a PCMH model within an organization can enhance the goals of quality care and improvement of patient centric outcomes, while also increasing privacy and security considerations.

The development of the PCMH model is a new objective of the PPACA that emphasizes meeting quality care standards in an organization, with focus on patient-centered outcomes. The Agency for Healthcare Research and Quality (AHRQ) defines PCMH as organizations that provide "primary healthcare that is relationship-based with an orientation toward the whole person" (AHRQ, 2013). They emphasize new and innovative forms of care, typically through evidence-based medicine and clinical decision-support tools. Patients are supposed to be the main focus of care, as opposed to meeting quotas or reimbursement objectives. There is efficient and timely access to physicians, and a systems-based approach of information sharing. Examples of PCMH practice redesign efforts may include "ongoing assistance from a change facilitator, ongoing consultation from a panel of experts in practice economics, health information technology, quality improvement, discounted software technology, training, and support" (Nutting et al., 2009). These objectives of the PCMH directly emphasize security and privacy of big data (Finkelstein et al., 2011). Finkelstein et al. present the PCMH and suggest how involvement of numerous stakeholders in a PCMH can pose advantages and disadvantages. The advantage is that HIPAA compliance of big data can produce a strengthened system of data storage and exchange across a large network of health information sharing, if all of the providers are HIPAA compliant. The PCMH also poses threats if an unsecured environment of big data is present in any one provider setting. Because the PCMH is completely cyber in infrastructure, it becomes very important for the consumer and the providers involved to be HIPAA compliant, and securely exchanging health information. By developing PCMH-specific criteria for the EMR and other health information technologies in the organization, there can be a movement toward safer and more secure big data practices and exchange of health information (Finkelstein et al., 2011). Because this topic is relatively new, few examples note the presence of PCMH and its success or failure with HIPAA compliance, but it is a research topic to be pursued further. In the next hypothesis, the author explores the presence of the health information exchange as an interorganization model for producing a privacy-enabled platform for big data.

**Hypothesis 3:** A cloud-based health information storage and sharing system may pose challenges to HIPAA compliance and big data security concerns at the organizational level.

The presence of a "cloud" through the use of electronic portals of health information has become more common in the health industry, as the Veterans Affairs (VA) and Department of Defense (DoD) hospitals already use the cloud, and many private organizations are shifting toward the cloud as well. The cloud poses advantages and disadvantages for organizations. The objective of a cloud is to ultimately facilitate the PCMH model, as discussed above, as well as a health information exchange (HIE) model, to easily transfer data from organization to organization. Some of the advantages of the cloud posed to organizations are the cost savings, because storage of information on the cloud may be more easily, efficiently, and inexpensively achieved (Yuan, 2012). Information across the cloud can be easily transported to a number of industries rather than being only used by one organization or one industry. For example, information may be transferred and communicated across insurance companies, public health reporting companies, for telemedicine purposes, analytics, businesses, and more. Yet, this causes some of the barriers to cloud usage due to the need for high levels of security of health information on a cloud platform, especially if information is being exchanged across HIPAA compliant and non-compliant users of data (Cisco Systems, 2012). Other barriers to the cloud for organizations have been "compliance with meaningful use, protecting patient privacy, and making sure their healthcare applications can interoperate with any of the dozens of applications that other members of the exchange may be using" (Cisco Systems, 2012). The most common cloud companies today are eClinical Works and Practice Fusion, which focus primarily on storage of health information rather than exchange of health information (Yuan, 2012).

While there is information on storage of health information on the cloud, there is only limited research on whether the cloud is a safe way to allow HIEs, or sharing of health information across a local area (Yuan, 2012). The objective of the HIE is to connect the regional-level data exchange through a Regional Health Information Organization (RHIO) that will provide HIE locally, and then, ideally, will connect all health providers nationally at a National Health Information Network (NHIN) level. Yuan discusses particular projects where the cloud has been used for HIE, including his own project, the Direct Project. The Direct Project is used, developed, and promoted by the government in facilitating open data exchange. The Direct Project provides strict security in email, with encrypted messages, as well as exchanges of health insurance forms, referrals, test results, and more. The presence of the

Direct Project and others similar in nature suggest the need for more big data strategies that are secure for HIE on the cloud.

The cloud poses the challenges of security and privacy, especially in data sharing, which is why the author hypothesizes that organizations will require more HIPAA-compliant HIEs, and information on secure HIEs. The emphasis should be on health information sharing as well as storage, because health information sharing requires an equally high (if not higher) level of security.

The meso-level challenges to big data primarily stem from the need for organizational policies and procedures that can strengthen big data storage, retrieval, and exchanges. The presence of strong organizational cultures focused on secure and HIPAA-compliant policies may improve the framework for big data. The presence of a PCMH model of practices also promotes a secure electronic framework with patient-centered outcomes. Finally, the use of the cloud is also a technique that can promote big data security and quality of care. Next, the author explores the micro-level consequences of big data sharing.

## Micro-Level Challenges to EMR Adoption

At the micro level, the sharing of big data may be impacted by consumer involvement in their personal records, and the presence of consumers on social media portals, Web portals, and discussion forums. Though information from large organizations and government entities may be HIPAA-compliant and deidentified, consumers may pose threats to their own security if they are not careful about the information that is posted about themselves on the Web. For this reason, the micro level focuses on the micro-level research question: What is the impact of consumer involvement in health records and health information on the state of big data? The hypotheses include the role of consumers in social media participation and its impact on big data, as well as the role of electronic health literacy and how consumers may affect their own quality of care and health through knowledge of the storage, access, and portals for their health records.

> **Research Question:** What is the effect of consumer involvement in health records and health information and the impact of consumer involvement on the state of big data?

> **Hypothesis 1:** Online user communities and social media may increase active participation in consumers' health choices and health information, while also increasing privacy and security risks to big data portals.

The use of the Web for information sharing, online user communities, and social media has become a revolution for patients and providers, because personal information about patients can be easily available and posted on the Web, and directly linked to their personal health records. For this reason, it is becoming important for providers to remain HIPAA compliant even when accessing Web portals and social media Web sites that may have personally identifiable health information posted by patients themselves.

van der Velden and Emam (2013) completed a study to see if teenage patients were posting personal, potentially identifiable, health information on social media Web sites. The study found that teenagers were not using the site for this purpose, but limitations of the study included primarily qualitative interviews of only 20 hospital patients. For this reason, more research on a larger sample size needs to be conducted to suggest whether various user groups of social media are posting private and confidential health information on social media sites and its impact for providers and other organizations. It also would be interesting to see the differences, if any, in the amount of personal health information between older and younger generations that use social media.

Examples of the use of patient forums suggest positive consequences of patient Web usage. The presence of forums like Patients Like Me have been useful in understanding how the Web helps patients with chronic conditions reach each other in new ways to develop support groups, relationships, and share health information (Wicks et al., 2010). Patients with some of the most serious illnesses were the most likely to share their personal information, suggesting an indirect relationship between fear of the Web, chronic illness, and information sharing. Patients were most likely to use the site for informed decision making and saw medical benefits as well (Wicks et al., 2010). For example, many patients found medication adherence to be a particular medical benefit as well as usage for diagnosis management and symptom management. Patient forums provide such benefits to data exchange, so it is difficult to deduce whether the costs of patient portals to big data security breaches may be worth the benefits to consumers and, potentially, to a secure big data portal in the long run.

There also are documented examples of patients misusing cell phones and laptops for sharing health information about other patients. A number of examples shed light on how serious the issue of security and privacy breaches through social networking and electronic media can be. For example, the University of California/Los Angeles neuropsychiatric hospital (UCLA) banned the usage of laptop and electronic devices (including cell phones) after a patient was caught posting pictures of other patients in the provider's office (Ornstein, 2008). The decision by the UCLA medical director was to be in favor of upholding privacy and confidentiality concerns, while also complying with California's patient law (Bitzer, 2012). Patients should be more careful about leaving any private health information, pictures, and evidence accessible to anyone on a Web page because this information could be used against them for a number of purposes, including big data research, filing of insurance claims, physician and provider reputation rankings, and clinical guidelines objectives, etc. Sites, such as Facebook and Gmail, own all information posted on their Web sites, which causes further complications in data usage. HIPAA still dictates that providers are in breach of the HIPAA Privacy Rule, even if a patient has posted his/her own information on the Web site and the provider is merely reading or accessing this information.

Detmer et al. (2008) discuss the implications of patient-controlled health records, also known as personal health records (PHRs), which promote integrated care delivery, decision making, and access benefits to patients of their health information. Of the various types of PHRs, including stand-alone, tethered, and integrated PHRs, Detmer et al. found that the integrated model was the most effective in improving "quality, completeness, depth, and accessibility" of health information for patients across exchanges of patients and providers, portability, and automation of content. Yet, consumers identified concerns with the use of PHRs because of fears of unauthorized access of their PHRs, unnecessary sharing of their information by providers through the electronic network, and the unfair access of insurance companies or third parties to their health information (Detmer et al., 2008). Despite the safeguards placed on PHRs by the Federal Trade Commission (FTC) rigid and final rules for PHR production and federal breach notification, there were nearly 11 million personal health record violations documented in the initial stages of the PHR rollout in the United States in 2008 (Redspin, 2011). Though the security and privacy breaches are important to the learning process to make the usage of personal health information better in the long run, the breaches place a high cost on big data security of patient information in the short run.

Some of the policy implications of personal health information security violations suggest that greater information needs to be provided to patients and health providers about the information they put on the Web and in their personal/mobile health record devices and how it could be used against them. There also is enough evidence to conclude that user communities, social media, and e-health are deriving benefits, even if it complicates the exchange of big data. This makes it difficult to assess whether benefits to patients outweigh potential costs to providers from accessing or seeing information that is not HIPAA compliant, but present on the Web. Discussed next is the effect of informed consent, or knowledge of patient choices in healthcare, which can provide important repercussions on what information is stored in big data. This can impact big data and quality of care in a number of settings.

> **Hypothesis 2:** Informed consent of consumers in their health decisions should increase the awareness of privacy concerns of exchanging information through the Web, while informed consent may decrease the risks posed to big data.

A focus on informed consent has become especially important since the introduction of HIPAA, electronic health records, and big data exchange in healthcare. Informed consent means that patients must "consent" to a working knowledge of what tests, treatments, procedures, and medical information they are being administered (Healthcare IT News, 2009). Informed consent also places emphasis on employees that are skilled in assessing whether a patient understands his or her own "health literacy, cultural, language, and family participation needs" in order to participate in a procedure. Informed consent plays an important role on big data because it will add to the policies required to comply with privacy concerns of big data. Informed consent involves large documents that are now being sent electronically to patients to provide them information on making health choices. The electronic storage of these documents will make it more difficult to validate that a patient did not know the health risks of particular procedures. Health IT News reports that some forms of informed consent are in systems, known as "best-of-breed systems," which provide "comprehensive libraries of procedure-specific consent documents," which can then be personalized by patient, surgical site, and information distinct to the patient's condition. The documents also are electronically available to a number of different individuals onsite, rather than a specific employee. Patients will now be able to more carefully understand the risks and challenges to treating health conditions and receiving health services, if they choose to pay attention to this information. They also can more easily contribute in the decision of whether or not they want their health information stored in particular ways by health providers, impacting the type of big data stored and used in health research.

A particular concern with informed consent in big data is the site 23 and Me, which received many criticisms, as discussed by Hayden (2012). The gene-testing company 23 and Me placed a patent on research for Parkinson's disease from gene sequences collected onsite. In this case, many consumers were complying with providing their health information, without reading policies on how it would be used. The fear that consumers have is that consent to research may mean problems for consumers later, because they are relinquishing their own data that was collected on them, deidentified or not. This example suggests more problems with informed consent—the difficulty for researchers, consumers/patients, and vendors of health portals in knowing if and how much data will be used about an individual, and whether it will be used in a protected manner. The policies that are written at the start of a project may be vague and lack transparency in what information the consumer is relinquishing and how the information may be used, primarily because the goals of the project may change after data collection. Hayden (2012) states potential solutions to big data problems through new technological systems like the BioVU databank at Vanderbilt University Medical Center, which differentiates data from DNA samples and the demographic data linked to the DNA sample. While the databases are linked, they are coded through a "synthetic derivative process," in which the data can no longer be linked to the patient's original identity. The example of the BioVU databank provides support for the types of new databases that may provide better deidentification of patient health information. The presence of informed consent plays an important role in micro-level health decisions and affects the kind of big data collection that may occur.

The two micro-level hypotheses suggest that social media and other electronic tools may be used by consumers for accessing and presenting health information. Informed consent provides consumers with information about the risks and benefits of exchange and storage of their health information in various portals, though transparency in informed consent still remains a challenge to big data. There are benefits and costs to consumers and providers in handling health information and ensuring compliance with HIPAA, informed consent, and other provisions linked to security and privacy concerns. Yet, the presence of such challenges also may produce improved solutions to big data challenges and may eventually lead to a secure electronic health system.

## Conclusion

The author introduced three levels of big data problems that may be evident in healthcare, including macro, meso, and micro challenges to big data. The macro-level research question discusses the challenges that the government faces in delivering HIPAA-compliant information for individuals and organizations. The author hypothesized that meeting HIPAA compliance standards may pose benefits and challenges to the deidentification of big data, and HIPAA compliance poses cyber security concerns for the health and health-related industry. The meso-level research question discusses the ways organizations can improve their information storage and retrieval of big data. The author hypothesized that organizations can make intraorganizational changes to meet security standards, organizations can use the patient-centered medical home models (PCMHs) of care to produce stronger security, and organizations may heighten their security risks through exchanging information across a cloud. The micro-level research question is regarding the presence of individual interest and decision making in Web-based platforms, including user online communities, social media, and PHRs, which impact big data. The presence of heightened information exchange through user online communities, social media, and PHRs may initially increase big data security concerns, though informed consent may aid in big data security challenges. The policy implications for the topics chosen suggest that, at the macro level, it will need greater enforcement and information sharing of HIPAA compliance standards along with industry support for security compliance. The policy implications for the meso changes include the need for new models of organizational management and culture to produce improved health outcomes, quality of care, and security standards in big data usage. Finally, policy implications for the micro challenges include the need for greater informed consent and health knowledge for patients and providers when using electronic portals for accessing and documenting their health information.

# References

Agency for Healthcare Research and Quality (AHRQ). 2013. PCMH definitions. Online at: http://www.pcmh.ahrq.gov/portal/server.pt/community/pcmh__home/1483

Agency for Healthcare Research and Quality (AHRQ). n.d. AHRQ fact sheet: Number of practicing primary care physicians in the United States. Online at: http://www.ahrq.gov/research/findings/factsheets/primary/pcwork1/index.html

Bitzer, W. 2012. HIPAA implications of social networking. Online at: http://www.alphca.com/uploadedFiles/aphca/Resource_Center/Events_and_Training/HIPAA%20and%20Social%20Networking%20Presentation%20-%20Windy%20Bitzer.pdf

Cisco Systems. 2012. Healthcare in the cloud: Health information exchanges and beyond. Online at: http://www.cisco.com/web/strategy/docs/gov/fedbiz031611Healthcare.pdf

Collmann, J., and T. Cooper. 2007. Breaching the security of the Kaiser Permanente Internet Patient Portal: The organizational foundations of information security. *Journal of the American Medical Informatics Association JAMIA* 14 (2): 239–243.

Detmer, D., M. Bloomrosen, B. Raymond, and P. Tang. 2008. Integrated personal health records: Transformative tools for consumer-centric care. *BMC Medical Informatics and Decision Making* 8 (1): 45.

El Emam, K., E. Jonker, L. Arbuckle, and B. Malin. 2011. A systematic review of re-identification attacks on health data. *PLoS ONE* 6 (12): e28071.

Finkelstein, J., M. S. Barr, P. P. Kothari, D. K. Nace, and M. Quinn. 2011. Patient-centered medical home cyberinfrastructure: Current and future landscape. *American Journal of Preventive Medicine* 40 (5) (Suppl. 2): S225–S233.

Hayden, C. 2012. Informed consent key. *Healthcare IT News.* Online at: http://www.healthcareitnews.com/news/informed-consent-key (accessed May 21, 2013).

Health and Human Services. 2012, 2013. Health information privacy case examples. Online at: http://www.hhs.gov/ocr/privacy/hipaa/enforcement/examples/allcases.html

Healthcare IT News. n.d. Proposed bill would expand telehealth services, bolster federal payouts. Online at: http://www.healthcareitnews.com/news/proposed-bill-would-expand-telehealth (accessed May 23, 2013).

Kwon, J., and M. E. Johnson. 2013. Security practices and regulatory compliance in the healthcare industry. *Journal of the American Medical Informatics Association* 20 (1): 44–51.

McGraw, D. 2012. Building public trust in uses of HIPAA de-identified data. Online at: https://mymasonportal.gmu.edu/bbcswebdav/pid-3158048-dt-content-rid-17385050_1/courses/13124.201310/J%20Am%20Med%20Inform%20Assoc-2013-McGraw-29-34.pdf?target = blank

McGraw, D., J. X. Dempsey, L. Harris, and J. Goldman. 2009. Privacy as an enabler, not an impediment: Building trust into health information exchange. *Health Affairs* 28 (2): 416–427.

Mercuri, R. T. 2004. The HIPAA-potamus in health care data security. *Communications of the ACM* 47 (7). Online at: http://www. notablesoftware.com/Papers/HIPAA.pdf

National Journal.com. Survey: Americans say health care reform isn't working … yet. n.d. Online at: http://www.nationaljour-nal.com/healthcare/survey-americans-say-health-care-reform-isn-t-working-yet-20110912 (accessed February 9, 2013).

Nutting, P. A., W. L. Miller, B. F. Crabtree, C.R. Jaen, E. E. Stewart, and K. C. Stange. 2009. Initial lessons from the first national demonstration project on practice transformation to a patient-centered medical home. *The Annals of Family Medicine* 7 (3): 254–260.

Ornstein, C. (2008, March 18). UCLA bans cellphones at hospital. *Los Angeles Times*. Retrieved from http://articles.latimes.com/2008/mar/18/local/me-ucla18

Redspin (blog). 2011. Preventing a healthcare data breach epidemic. Online at: http://www.redspin.com/blog/2011/07/01/preventing-a-healthcare-data-breach-epidemic/

van der Velden, M., and K. E. Emam. 2013. Not all my friends need to know: A qualitative study of teenage patients, privacy, and social media. *Journal of the American Medical Informatics Association* 20 (1): 16–24.

Wicks, P., M. Massagli, J. Frost, C. Brownstein, S. Okun, T. Vaughan, … J. Heywood. 2010. Sharing health data for better outcomes on PatientsLikeMe. *Journal of Medical Internet Research* 12 (2).

Yuan, M. J. 2012, Nov. The direct project: Sending health information over the cloud. Online at: http://www.ibm.com/developerworks/library/cl-directproject/

# Chapter 9

# Geographic Disparities in Healthcare

## Chapter Summary

The United States is a melting pot of cultures, races, ethnicities, and has a wide variation in demographics across the country. The Institute of Medicine (IOM) has completed a review of the minority populations in the United States and found that there are disparities in the distribution of health resources for ethnic minorities in this country because of the location of minorities and their accessibility to healthcare resources (Baicker, Chandra, and Skinner, 2005). The author's essay focuses primarily on such geographic disparities in health resources and healthcare services (with services focused on primary care physicians), to provide potential policy solutions to overcome the geographic disparities. The author analyzes some papers that discuss racial inequities in particular locations, as well as general economic disparities, but focuses primarily on disparities in the supply of health resources and supply of health services within specific geographic contexts (regions and neighborhoods). While there are also theories linked to inequality in health literacy rates across these populations, the discussion focuses on the supply side, which is the provision of health resources and services by health providers to various geographical regions.

In the first section, the author documents the major challenges in providing health resources across geographic regions and to the areas of highest need. In the second section, the shortages in health professionals, specifically physicians, in specific geographic areas are discussed. Then the focus is on three policy solutions, the first of which the U.S. government has currently proposed to ameliorate the shortage of healthcare resources, services, and professionals in various geographic regions. The first policy solution is the creation of community health centers (CHCs), federally qualified health centers (FQHCs), and other government clinics that may be located in areas that are geographically underserved. This policy solution is being enforced through the Patient Protection and Affordable Care Act (PPACA) and through government grants. The second policy solution is not yet enforced through government means, but has been carried out successfully—the introduction of telemedicine and technologies to improve health resources and service delivery to areas of geographic disparity. The final solution provided is very new, known as concierge medicine, which also may provide benefits if this form of care relocates to areas of geographic need. The author concludes with remarks on the subject and how we can utilize all three solutions to improve the status of our healthcare system.

# Geographic Disparities in Health Resources

The Department of Health and Human Services (DHHS) reported in 1985 that minorities were consistently appearing to have worse health outcomes and rankings due to a number of nongenetic factors. This fact has gained considerable evidence to date. Some of the factors that may be impacting communities with disparities include patient location in relation to access to health insurance and services, personal choice in the utilization of health resources within a location (e.g., due to immigration patterns), and the "neighborhood effect," which can include the economic status of a neighborhood and quality of care in the region. Discussed are articles that link geography to disparities in access and equity to health resources and quality of care.

Anderson et al. (2004) discuss the reasons for limited research on geographic disparities in healthcare. They note three underlying points that play a role in the limited nature of geographic disparity research. There are three major confounding problems with geographic disparities research: (1) there is variation in utilization and outcomes for patients, by region; (2) patients of color tend to visit physicians and services that match their background for utilizing healthcare on a regular basis, compared to patients who are not of color; and (3) racial disparities are more common in some geographic areas than others, making an uneven state of health outcomes. These factors tend to interact and make the study of geographic disparities even more difficult, as there is no clear way to know whether demand or supply drives patient preferences and the supply, quality, access, and utilization patterns of hospital resources and services.

Chandra and Skinner (2003) also document major reasons for geographic disparities in healthcare, which includes matters of utilization, personal choice, supplier (physician) distribution, quality of care differences, and regional differences in treatment and outcomes.

The authors analyzed their study of utilization and personal choice in greater detail, and then used Morenoff and Lynch (2002) to discuss regional differences in treatment and outcomes. (In the next section (Geographic Disparities in Healthcare Professionals), physician distribution differences across geography are discussed.)

Chandra and Skinner (2003) provide a statistical analysis of the utilization of hospitals by cardiovascular patients, after controlling for a number of confounding variables that could affect the research (patient migration to hospitals, sampling problems with Medicaid patients that are not representative of the population due to severe illnesses, and random noise generated by average rates of healthcare usage across state boundaries). They find that health utilization actually varies regardless of health status; health status in a region was not statistically significant in its association with health utilization, but health disparities existed in utilization across geography (at a statistically significant level, which is not documented). Some of the reasons Chandra and Skinner provide for the underlying disparity in utilization of healthcare across the United States for cardiovascular disease patients include: "the differences in underlying severity of the disease, patient preferences, the role of capacity of services, and the nature of physician learning in different areas." The practice and "intensity" of medicine, measured as readmission rates, varies across geography, especially within states and cities. Racial differences in migration patterns of patients to the hospitals also signified differences in utilization and health.

Chandra and Skinner (2003) also acknowledge differences in insurance status and health provider utilization by race and geography. For example, they utilize the National Bureau of Economic Research Medicare claims data to plot the relationship between hospital readmissions and race, which suggests that areas with higher rates of minorities (in this case, African Americans) had higher rates of hospital readmissions. They also suggest that this is not indicative of health resource utilization alone, but may be affected by where a concentration of minorities lives, in relation to the hospital that has high readmission rates. Similarly, Lillie-Blanton, Martinez, and Salganicoff (2001) find that emergency room visits were higher by minorities in some geographic areas more so than others. The supply (and quality) of emergency room and hospital care may require greater attention, along with higher numbers of hospital beds, based on populations within a geography. The utilization of healthcare and choice of healthcare resources by minorities in particular geographic regions may need more research to document the patterns of choice.

Horev, Pesis-Katz, and Mukamel (2004) analyzed the disparity in health resources, such as the number of hospital beds across the United States, as well as the number of physicians in various locations, across a historical period. Their findings suggest that the physician distribution has become less equitable over time, except for the West Coast, though the number of hospital beds at the county level has increased as needed for each geographic segment of the population. The limitation of the study is that rates of beds per capita may not be enough to understand the association between the number of beds and the equality in bed distribution. Their paper could be explored further to understand how many other factors, such as type of hospital, technologies at the hospital, and types of physicians (primary care, specialty, concierge care) could impact the geographic distribution of resources and services.

Morenoff and Lynch (2002) analyzed the theory of neighborhoods that may impact disparities in health, focusing on aging populations. They use the term *neighborhood effects,* which is the "study of how local context influences the health and well-being of individuals in a way that cannot be reduced to the properties of the individuals themselves." They note that there are more reasons for the disparities in healthcare that reach beyond the individual level or the "ecological niche" where a particular immigrant or racial/ethnic population may be born. While poverty, socioeconomic status, race, and health status may be tied together, there needs to be research that conducts multilevel analysis focusing on neighborhood effects.

Alter et al. (1999), Garg, Diener-West, and Powe (2001), and Iwashyna, Christakis, and Becker (1999) analyzed health services disparities using the "neighborhood effect." Alter et al. analyzed neighborhood income to suggest whether the neighborhood has an effect on the access to invasive cardiac procedures and the mortality rate one year after the procedure for myocardial infarction. They found that increases in neighborhood income were linked to a 23% increase in usage of the cardiac procedures and caused a 45% decrease in wait times in neighborhoods with higher incomes. Using survival analysis, they also found that an increase in income of $10,000 led to a 10% lower risk of death at a $p < 0.01$ level of significance. Garg, Diener-West, and Powe analyzed the effect of racially diverse neighborhoods on the supply of cardiopulmonary resuscitation (CPR). After conducting a multivariate logistic regression analysis of 4,379 cardiac arrests in Chicago from 1998 to 1999, they found that there was variation in the rate of CPR delivered, based on neighborhood characteristics, such as racially integrated neighborhoods. Cardiac arrests were more likely to get CPR treatment if they occurred in racially integrated neighborhoods or all white neighborhoods rather than all black neighborhoods. Similarly, in-home cardiac arrests and middle-aged black residents (at an individual level) received fewer CPR treatments. Another study by Iwashyna, Christakis, and Becker suggests that neighborhoods in lower socioeconomic conditions were less likely to be placed on the renal transplant waiting list, and had higher chances of mortality. The effect of private insurance coverage and Medicare also increases the chance of getting wait-listed for transplantation. These studies that employ the neighborhood effect suggest that there are socioeconomic influences of the neighborhood that can impact the type of health services received, and also may impact healthcare delivery, health professionals providing care in the area, and other factors. The studies do not specify whether national and state taxpayer dollars, local taxes and grants, economic resources in the region, and salaries of families living in particular neighborhoods may be highly correlated with the neighborhood effect as well.

The examples in this section suggest that healthcare resources, such as hospital beds, utilization of resources, quality of resources, and access to various healthcare treatments (heart attack, CPR, end-stage kidney disease (ESRD) transplants) are affected by some individual characteristics as well as various neighborhood effects, racial disparities across geography, socioeconomic status, and patterns of minority health utilization in a region. Next, the author explores the effect of geography on the supply of health professionals in the community.

# Geographic Disparities in Healthcare Professionals

This section discusses the health professional shortages across geographic regions and its impact on the community. A number of examples of primary care professionals and physicians in different settings are analyzed, including rural health and pediatric health. Also provided are reasons for why the distribution of health professionals is skewed in some areas.

While nearly one-fifth of the U.S. population lives in rural areas, only 10% of the U.S.'s physicians practice in rural areas, causing rural America to be particularly affected by the shortage in primary care physicians. Fewer physicians settle in rural areas because urban areas offer them more flexibility, higher compensation, career growth, and other perks. Rural areas also tend to have individuals without health insurance, which disincentivizes the primary care professionals from practicing in rural areas based on the likelihood of lower reimbursement rates from managed care programs (Rosenblatt and Hart,

2000). Family practice physicians are much more likely to practice in rural areas than specialists, which makes the access to specialists another major priority for rural communities. The unenticing quality of life in rural areas for health professionals leads them to settle in urban areas, causing a geographic disparity in the amount of healthcare provided to individuals residing in rural communities.

Another article by the American Academy of Family Physicians (AAFP) suggests that family practice physicians, though facing shortages in rural areas, are actually the main point of contact for many rural communities. The creation of more medical programs that recruit individuals from rural communities for rural medical programs may increase the number of family practice physicians that have a desire to remain in rural areas after graduation. There are disparities even across "large rural areas," "small rural areas," and "isolated rural areas," as the number of family practice physicians practicing in large rural areas is highest at 11%, and the number of family practice physicians is lowest in the isolated rural areas at 4% (AAFP, 2012). These numbers are even lower for pediatricians, as about 6% of all pediatricians reside in large rural areas, whereas only 0.8% of pediatricians reside in isolated rural areas. The numbers demonstrate the need for physicians across rural areas, and how there is variation even within rural areas (AAFP, 2012).

Shipman et al. (2010) analyzed the geographic distribution of primary care professionals for children and pediatricians between 1996 and 2006. Their data suggests that nearly 1 million children were living in areas without local physicians and almost all 50 states had the same ratio of physician maldistribution. They recommend that greater accountability needs to occur for specific funding purposes of physician training toward pediatric populations and should reduce the disparity in the ratio of physicians reaching children's populations.

Along with the maldistribution of primary care and specialty physicians, the number of female and minority physicians in rural and certain geographic areas also are problematic. The AAFP and Rosenblatt and Hart (2000) suggest the lack of minority and female physicians in rural areas, which has been a historical trend for many decades. Only about 15% of physicians are females, and fewer than 5% are minorities. The study shows that minority physicians are more likely to practice in rural areas or areas with higher levels of minorities. The study also found that African Americans were more likely to cater to Medicaid patients, and Hispanics were likely to cater to uninsured patients. Today, greater recruitment is occurring to increase the numbers of minorities that are practicing, which can provide for a balance in the inequities in distribution of health professional services.

The following examples suggest some of the disparities associated with physicians practicing in certain geographic areas and for populations living in particular communities. Rural areas, populations of minorities, and pediatric populations lack a proper supply of professionals, which impacts the delivery and access to health services for these populations. The next section details some of the current policy solutions to reduce the problems being faced by the populations impacted by a geographic inequity in resources and care.

# Policy Solutions to Geographic Maldistribution of Resources and Care

The following section provides three policy solutions to the problems of health resource and health professional delivery and presence in certain geographic areas. The policy solutions include the presence of government health centers (FQHCs, CHCs), telemedicine and telehealth technologies, and concierge medicine.

## Solutions to the Shortage of Health Resources and Services: Federally Qualified Health Centers (FQHCs) and Community Health Centers (CHCs)

New data on geographic disparities and geographic need for primary care physicians may facilitate more research on how to combat the imbalance of resources and physicians to certain geographic areas and populations. Petterson et al. (2012) also suggest that "geographic maldistribution" has led to problems in primary care shortages, which require "specific policies regarding training, recruitment, and retention" in the necessary areas. The proposed policy solution currently is to counter the lack of primary care physicians in rural areas through federal funding of $11 billion in the next five years, toward community health centers, federally qualified health centers, and other federally funded clinics. The government also has passed a program called the National Health Service Corps that supports the funding of health professional shortage areas (HPSAs), and has supported funding to federally qualified health centers (FQHCs) and community health centers (CHCs) in order to promote primary care access to populations in geographic need.

Rosenblatt and Hart (2000) suggest government programs that have aided in health professional shortage problems across rural areas, including the National Health Service Corps (NHSC) and the CHC. The NHSC produces programs including the designation of HPSAs, which are provided funding from the government to aid these areas. The Section 332 of the Public Health Service Act includes information on the designation of HPSAs, which are facilities that must fit specific guidelines of need (such as low-income populations, rural classification, distinct minority population visitation areas) set by the secretary of DHHS to be eligible for funding, training, and resources. There are three types of HPSA designations: HPSA facilities, population groups, and geographic areas (counties). There are also three types of HPSAs: mental health, dental, and primary care HPSAs, which fill the gap in resources documented in the previous section. This policy can impact the presence of resources and physicians, along with the presence of government providers of healthcare.

Research by the National Association of Community Health Centers (NACHC) on FQHCs and CHCs suggest the ability of the two types of government health centers to impact nearly one in seven rural residents in a number of ways. Some of these include:

- Providing high need areas with health professions, especially areas associated with the worst health indicators for infant mortality
- Offering transportation, health education, case management, and home visit services for patients to access health care
- Tailoring services to minorities, cultural enclaves, and specific communities

Patients attending these government health centers have seen benefits, including higher rates of rural female patients that receive pap smears than rural females nationally, patients with fewer low birth weight babies, patients in areas with 25% fewer population visiting the emergency department, and an estimated $5 billion in economic returns from greater jobs, goods, and services from rural health centers (NACHC, 2011).

The importance of making family practice and specialty practice more enticing for professionals practicing in rural areas and in recruiting professionals that have knowledge of rural community health (by being natives of the region) may reduce disparities in health across rural communities. The current policies in the United States provide funding and programs for government health centers in rural areas and areas of need, which only targets a deficiency of resources in the areas of geographic need. A few of these programs include health centers in HPSAs and the presence of CHCs and FQHCs. New policy initiatives need to consider incentives to recruit professionals that are willing to practice in rural areas. The next set of solutions utilize telemedicine to impact the geographic maldistribution of services and resources.

## Solutions to the Shortage of Health Resources and Services: Telemedicine Resources

The World Health Organization (WHO) defines telemedicine as "the use of information communication technologies (ICT) to improve patient outcomes by increasing access to care and medical information" (WHO, 2009). A number of studies document the use of telemedicine to counter problems faced by populations in rural areas from shortages of resources and health professionals. No federal policies mandate the use of telemedicine in health provider settings, though a new bill was introduced, called the Telehealth Promotion Act of 2012 (H.R. 6719), sponsored by Rep. Mike Thompson (D-CA). This bill may increase federal payments and interest in telehealth services across Medicare, Medicaid, Children's Health Insurance Programs, TRICARE, other federal employee health plans and the Department of Veterans Affairs. This bill would create a national reimbursement policy that would permit reimbursing services that utilize telemedicine. The literature suggests some administrative and reimbursement hassles with telemedicine, though the strengths of telemedicine provide access to chronic health needs of disparate populations.

Rosenblatt and Hart (2000) recommend telemedicine for communities in rural areas because of the benefits to access healthcare across geographic areas, lower reimbursement rates by third-party providers, and likelihood that physicians will participate due to fewer problems with travel and reduced costs on duplication of tests from an electronic system. Hilty et al. (2008) documents the presence of telepsychiatry in rural areas, which can improve access to many patients and serve minorities that are typically not reached in these areas. Their recommendation is the need for greater training in telemedicine specialty programs for providers of telemedicine care. Similarly, Saler, Switzer, and Hess (2011) analyze the effect of telemedicine to improve stroke care in remote locations. They find that stroke specialists are able to conduct all the normal processes that they would have done in person, including examining patients and reviewing image with detailed decisions. They find that telestroke networks are a good solution to acute care treatment programs in remote areas. Pedigo and Odoi (2010) use GIS (geographic information systems) to analyze the disparities in geographic accessibility to stroke and myocardial infarction in East Tennessee. They found that nearly 8 to 15% of populations did not have access to myocardial infarction (MI) or stroke care, though air ambulance and telemedicine serve as excellent techniques in reaching these populations. These studies suggest that telemedicine is valuable for geographic disparities, especially for rural communities with chronic and mental health conditions, including psychiatry, stroke, and MI.

Some studies also document the presence of telemedicine in Medicaid majority areas, such as a study by Gray et al. (2006). They analyzed states that participated in Medicaid telemedicine reimbursement programs, and found that 17 of the 25 states using these programs did not provide reimbursement. Many administrative issues complicate the presence of telemedicine, including provider and reimbursement complications and cost-benefit analysis that were conducted. The study found that telemedicine was useful in these Medicaid (low income) majority areas, but faced problems in the administration. These administrative hassles support the idea that policy makers must consider an easier method to reduce reimbursement and administrative hassle of telemedicine usage.

Telemedicine has been depicted as having a beneficial impact on chronic, mental health, and diseased populations that lack access to health resources due to geographic disparities (Hilty et al., 2008; Saler, Switzer, and Hess, 2011; Pedigo and Odoi, 2010). Yet, no official government telemedicine policy provides reimbursement or incentives for telemedicine usage thus far. The author suggests concierge medicine as a possible solution, because it may counter many of the problems that have been associated so far with telemedicine usage in the populations with geographic disparities. Next, concierge medicine is analyzed as a policy solution to the shortage of resources and professionals in areas of geographic disparity.

## Solutions to the Shortage of Health Resources and Services: Concierge Medicine

Concierge medicine focuses on a patient-centered model of healthcare, utilizing technology as an innovative aspect of the organization, with the objective of improved quality of care outcomes for patients. The use of telemedicine in concierge practices is common, and it is likely that mobile health and electronic health record technologies also may be used by these populations (Knope, 2010). Considering that these physicians utilize health technologies and do not require complicated reimbursement functions with third-party payers, concierge medicine may be a valuable solution, if these physicians promote their care in areas of geographic disparity.

The problems faced by individuals living in rural areas can be solved by having more concierge physicians work in rural areas, because they do not need health insurance reimbursement and may be more likely than traditional physicians to cater to populations without insurance or to populations paying out of pocket. On the other hand, the populations in these regions may underutilize healthcare, making concierge medicine less promising in these areas. Literature suggests that the majority of concierge physicians have training in family medicine or internal medicine, and have been hospitalists in the past (MedPAC, 2010). An article that interviews American Academy of Pediatrics member and speaker Chip Hart suggests that many pediatricians are switching to concierge medicine (AAPP, 2013). This makes them a potentially good fit for regions with populations that have been overutilizing emergency rooms, and require attention from family practice and prevention-based care.

A report by the Concierge Medicine Research Collective and Concierge Medicine News (2013) provides results that could affect concierge medicine in areas with geographic disparities. The report found that patients in rural areas were not finding concierge care, though there was demand for this style of care. On the other hand, in some states, such as Virginia, Pennsylvania, Florida, and California, concierge care was prevalent at higher rates, meeting the demand by patients. The report was not clear as to the specific form of concierge care, be it fee for service, fee for care, or hybrid models of care. More research in this arena will help decipher the difference that concierge medicine can make on the supply and demand because the type of care being provided varies by insurance accepted by the state, state laws on practicing concierge medicine, and regulations.

Concierge Medicine Research Collective and Concierge Medicine News also documented the fastest-growing cities with concierge medicine. The cities included Los Angeles, San Francisco, New York, Palm Beach, and Baltimore among the top five in the United States. To solidify these poll projections, a study by Merritt Hawkins & Associates also provides information on doctors considering concierge-style practices. The company stated that the highest percentage considering the new business model was in Texas, at nearly 10.6%, followed by Florida, 9.1%; New York, 8.0%; and California, 6.7%. Pennsylvania was at 4.5% and at the bottom of the list. By diverting these physicians to working in the rural and low-income communities within these states, it is a possibility that concierge medicine may have a pronounced impact on geographic disparities.

A potential way to incentivize the concierge physicians is to provide compensation for meeting quality of care objectives that are part of the patient-centered medical home (PCMH) model. The PPACA proposes a PCMH model of care that focuses on prevention-based outcomes through an innovative practice design and indicators to reach positive health benchmarks. The PCMH model provides financial incentives to physicians to meet certain criteria, as a capitation on top of their normal earnings and reimbursement structure. These measures can translate into better health outcomes for populations, while also providing incentives to the physicians for using a standard for practicing care. The physicians would not need to alter their current reimbursement mechanisms, but would receive a capitation (retainer) for achieving particular objectives.

The discussion on concierge medicine is hypothetical, but provides a solution to the current shortage of health resources and professional services in certain geographic communities. Concierge medicine physicians are typically family practice physicians or pediatricians, who are potentially good fits for the need in rural and underprivileged communities. These physicians also are unburdened by administrative and billing hassles, which typically is the problem for physicians that have to practice telemedicine in rural and underserved communities. Concierge physicians currently primarily serve urban areas, but changes in federal and state policies could help promote more physicians practicing in areas of need.

## Conclusion

This chapter analyzed the supply of health resources and professionals in geographic areas of need, and discussed the major problems being faced due to geographic disparity. The author found that health resources are primarily underutilized by certain populations, demographics, and ethnicities, and a *neighborhood effect* prevails in certain communities. The neighborhood effect includes economic and racial differences at the county level, which impacts specific health services received. When analyzing health professional shortages, the author found that primary care and pediatrics are an important need, and female and minority professionals are also a priority in certain geographic areas. The author researched potential policy solutions and found that the first policy solution is already being conducted by the United States, which is the funding of community health centers and federally qualified health centers. The second policy solution of telemedicine is being evaluated by the U.S. Medicare and Medicaid programs, though it is already being used privately by many hospitals and has shown beneficial results in aiding geographic health needs, especially for chronic conditions. Finally, a new solution of concierge medicine was proposed, which may combine the first two solutions to provide innovative healthcare at a lower cost. The main focus should be on moving concierge care to areas of geographical need in order to enhance performance and improve health outcomes for these communities. The policies suggested looked primarily at the supply side of healthcare, analyzing the shortage of health resources and professionals in areas of geographic disparity. The impact of such policies affect the future of the U.S. health system.

# References

American Academy of Family Physicians (AAFP). 2012. Data illustrate geographic dispersal of family physicians, other primary care professionals. Online at: http://www.aafp.org/online/en/home/publications/news/news-now/practice-professional-issues/20120203ahrqgeodata.html

American Academy of Family Physicians (AAFP). n.d. Facts about ACOs. Online at: http://www.aafp.org/online/en/home/practicemgt/specialtopics/designs/practiceaffiliationoptions/faq.html

Alter, D. A., C. D. Naylor, P. Austin, and J. V. Tu. 1999. Effects of socioeconomic status on access to invasive cardiac procedures and on mortality after acute myocardial infarction. *The New England Journal of Medicine* 341 (18): 1359–1367.

Anderson, N. B., R. A. Bulatao, and B. Cohen. eds. 2004. *Critical perspectives on racial and ethnic differences in health in late life*. Washington, D.C.: National Academies Press. Online at: http://www.ncbi.nlm.nih.gov/books/NBK25532/

Baicker, K., A. Chandra, and J. S. Skinner. 2005. Geographic variation in health care and the problem of measuring racial disparities. *Perspectives in Biology and Medicine* 48 (1 Suppl), S42–53.

Chandra, A., and J. Skinner. 2003. *Geography and racial health disparities*. (Working paper no. 9513). Cambridge, MA: National Bureau of Economic Research. Online at: http://www.nber.org/papers/w9513

*Concierge Medicine News*. 2013. Demand for concierge medical care currently outweighs supply of physicians across U.S. Online at: http://conciergemedicinenews.wordpress.com/2013/01/16/demand-for-concierge-medical-care-currently-outweighs-supply-of-physicians-across-u-s/ (accessed March 29, 2013).

Garg, P. P., M. Diener-West, and N. R. Powe. 2001. Income-based disparities in outcomes for patients with chronic kidney disease. *Seminars in Nephrology* 21 (4): 377–385.

Gray, G. A., B. H. Stamm, S. Toevs, U. Reischl, and D. Yarrington. 2006. Study of participating and nonparticipating states' telemedicine Medicaid reimbursement status: Its impact on Idaho's policymaking process. *Telemedicine Journal and e-Health: The official Journal of the American Telemedicine Association* 12 (6): 681–690.

Hilty, D. M., H. C. Cobb, J. D. Neufeld, J. A. Bourgeois, and P. M. Yellowlees. 2008. Telepsychiatry reduces geographic physician disparity in rural settings, but is it financially feasible because of reimbursement? *The Psychiatric Clinics of North America* 31 (1): 85–94.

Horev, T., I. Pesis-Katz, and D. B. Mukamel. 2004. Trends in geographic disparities in allocation of health care resources in the U.S. *Health Policy* (Amsterdam, Netherlands) 68 (2): 223–232.

Iwashyna, T. J., N. A. Christakis, and L. B. Becker. 1999. Neighborhoods matter: A population-based study of provision of cardiopulmonary resuscitation. *Annals of Emergency Medicine* 34 (4, Pt 1): 459–468.

Knope, S. D. 2010. *Concierge medicine: A new system to get the best healthcare*. Lanham, MD: Rowman & Littlefield.

Lillie-Blanton, M., R. M. Martinez, and A. Salganicoff. 2001. Site of medical care: Do racial and ethnic differences persist? *Yale Journal of Health Policy, Law, and Ethics* 1, 15–32.

MedPAC. 2010. Contractor report: Retainer-based physicians: Characteristics, impact, and policy considerations. Online at: http://www.medpac.gov/documents/oct10_retainerbasedphysicians_contractor_cb.pdf

Morenoff, J., and J. Lynch. 2002. What makes a place healthy? Neighborhood influences on racial/ethnic disparities in health over the life course. Paper presented at the National Academy of Science, Health Disparities and Aging Symposium, Washington, D.C.

National Association of Community Health Centers (NACHC). 2011. Removing barriers to care: Community health centers in rural areas. Online at: http://www.nachc.com/client/documents/Rural%20Fact%20Sheet%20-%20November%202011.pdf

Pedigo, A. S., and A. Odoi. 2010. Investigation of disparities in geographic accessibility to emergency stroke and myocardial infarction care in East Tennessee using geographic information systems and network analysis. *Annals of Epidemiology* 20 (12): 924–930.

Rosenblatt, R. A., and L. G. Hart. 2000. Physicians and rural America. *Western Journal of Medicine* 173 (5): 348–351.

Saler, M., J. A. Switzer, and D. C. Hess. 2011. Use of telemedicine and helicopter transport to improve stroke care in remote locations. *Current Treatment Options in Cardiovascular Medicine* 13 (3): 215–224.

Shipman, S., J. Lan, C. Chang, and D. Goodman. 2010. Geographic maldistribution of primary care for children. *Pediatrics*.

World Health Organization (WHO). 2009. *Telemedicine: Opportunities and development in member states* (Global Observatory for eHealth Series, 2). Geneva, Switzerland: World Health Organization. Online at: http://www.who.int/goe/publications/goe_telemedicine_2010.pdf

## Chapter 10

# International Comparisons: Differences in U.K. and U.S. Preventive Health

## Chapter Summary

The objective of this chapter is to produce a comparative perspective on the U.K. and U.S. health systems, specifically analyzing reforms made by the United Kingdom in primary care during the early 2000s. The author provides a short overview of the U.K. and U.S. health systems and produces comparisons and contrasts between the systems, as well as trends in the general practitioner (GP) and specialist populations of the United Kingdom and United States. The author then provides examples of the newest changes that have occurred to the primary care system in the U.K.'s National Health Services (NHS) in the early 2000s, using an article by Doran and Roland (2010) and others, and provides examples of how this has applied and may improve some objectives for the United States. After this, the author analyzes a new policy solution, the presence of concierge medicine* in the United States, and compares some of the strategies being used by the United Kingdom for its GP population to the U.S.'s concierge medicine system. The author utilizes some interesting new solutions of telemedicine and health information technologies that concierge physicians are able to incorporate into their practice of medicine. The author concludes with remarks on what can be learned from comparisons of the U.K. and U.S. health systems, and where the United States could potentially apply the lessons from the U.K.'s health reforms.

# Applying the Reforms of the U.K. NHS to the U.S. Health System: A Comparative Perspective

## Introduction

Many of the most industrialized nations have grown by reforming their health systems in unique ways. The United Kingdom is one such industrialized nation that has undergone numerous reforms, including one particular reform in the early 2000s that suggests positive and negative health outcomes. Because the United States has recently introduced the Patient Protection and Affordable Care Act (PPACA), which creates a single-payer system, it may be of importance to compare the new single-payer system of the United States to the long-standing U.K. health system and U.K.'s recent reform. This may guide the United States on how specific reforms in the United Kingdom have had strengths and weaknesses in implementation. In order to make such comparisons between the U.S. and U.K. health systems, especially postreform, it is important to understand each health system under a historical context. Each country's history shapes its objectives and health outcomes.

## General Differences: The U.K. versus the U.S. Health System

The U.K. and U.S. health systems have different histories that shape their healthcare objectives and the presence of primary care in each country today. The author provides a short overview of differences in the health systems and the primary care labor force before discussing the new initiatives taken by the United Kingdom and the United States in the early 2000s, toward improved quality of care. The United Kingdom has a number of publicly funded health systems, including the National Health Service (NHS), Health and Social Care in Northern Ireland (HSCNI), NHS Scotland, and NHS Wales. The author primarily focuses on comparisons between the U.K. NHS, the largest of the four publicly funded systems in the kingdom, and the U.S.'s health system. The NHS has been publicly funded through taxpayer dollars since its early beginnings in the 1940s (NHS, 2013). On the other hand, the U.S. health system has been funded through private insurance companies, HMO programs, and employer-funded insurance since its early beginnings in the 1900s. The two countries have varying levels of health risk factors, though they are close in life expectancy measures, at about 80 years of life expectancy. Taking into account many of the differences across the U.K. and U.S. health system, which stem from their histories and the way the systems are funded, the next section discusses the differences in the U.S. and U.K. primary care workforce. It explores comparisons in the new measures that were introduced in the U.K. health system, primarily in favor of improving the state of the GP population in the United Kingdom. The United States has had far fewer policies that are similar to the United Kingdom in the GP sector, possibly because the United Kingdom has focused on prevention and the GP population since its early beginnings. The United States has now proposed more focus on prevention and primary care, through the PPACA, though its efforts still lag behind the United Kingdom.

Because of the differences in population size between the two countries, the scale for the GP population in the United Kingdom, which is estimated at about 40,000, differs greatly from the United States, which is at about 210,000 primary care physicians (PCPs) (NHS, 2013; AHRQ, 2012). Regardless of size, the ratio of the GP to specialist populations in both countries differ. *The Huffington Post* reports that the mix between primary care and specialists is unbalanced in the United States, as nearly 70% of all physicians in the United States are specialists, and 30 percent are primary care physicians (*The Huffington Post*, 2010). This has increased the U.S.'s need for primary care physicians now, and in the future. The General Medical Council of the United Kingdom suggests that these numbers are more balanced for the U.K. ratio of primary care to specialists, at around 55% GP to 45% specialists (General Medical Council, 2013). When studying comparisons of referral rates for specialty care between the United States and United Kingdom, Forrest (2002) suggests that the referral rate for patients from primary care physicians to specialty care is about 35% in the United States, in comparison to only about 13% in the United Kingdom. The higher level referral of patients to specialty care in the U.S. managed care programs suggests the emphasis on specialty care over primary care in this country compared to the United Kingdom.

The Organization of Economic Cooperation and Development (OECD) provides comparisons of spending between the United Kingdom and United States for 2010. The United Kingdom spends about 40% of the U.S.'s health spending per capita, in that the United Kingdom spends only about $3,500 (adjusted on a per capita basis) compared to the United States, at about $8,200 per capita in 2010. Nearly 83% of the spending in the United Kingdom came from public sector funding in 2010, compared to about 48% of spending directly from the public sector in the United States (OECD, 2012). The United Kingdom has 2.7 physicians per 1,000 population, compared to the United States, which has 2.4 physicians per 1,000 population. This difference is surprising, considering the high level of U.S. per capita spending, which should account for higher labor quantity as well as costs.

The OECD Health Working Paper No. 41 of 2008 suggests differences in remuneration between GPs in the United States and United Kingdom. The United States has traditionally paid GPs the most in salary compared to other OECD nations, but the numbers are close to that of the United Kingdom. For example, the OECD Working Paper suggests that, in 2004, the average GP in the United States is paid about 3.4 times the average U.S. worker, in comparison to the average GP in the United Kingdom, who is paid about 3.1 times the average U.K. worker. These numbers are changing due to new policies in the United Kingdom in recent years from the pay-for-performance system (discussed in detail in the next section). The GP population of the United Kingdom has had a nearly 21% increase in its remuneration in 2004, after pay-for-performance, and nearly 10% in the years after that (OECD, 2008). The U.K. specialists also have seen targeted increases of about 5% in remuneration ever since the new pay-for-performance measures were initiated. On the other hand, the United States has seen decreases in remuneration for GPs of about 5%, due to reduction in Medicare and private payment systems in recent years, and similar stagnation for specialists in remuneration rates.

Yet, the United States has traditionally had one of the highest remuneration rates for specialists, as specialists receive about five times the average worker's remuneration. The role of specialists in the United States remains more lucrative and coveted than that of the U.S. GP, especially when the remuneration rates are not increasing over time. The United

Kingdom was noted to be one of the countries with the lowest gap in remuneration between GPs and specialists, which may account for why the United Kingdom does not have the pronounced shortage in the primary care workforce that the United States has. These proclaimed differences in financial reimbursement and interest in primary care workforce may contribute to many of the differences in policies in recent years for the U.S. and U.K. health systems, which is explored more in the next section.

# Reforms to the U.K. Health System in the Early 2000s

The early 2000s have spurred changes in the U.S. and U.K. NHS healthcare systems. The author first provides a discussion of some of the major changes in the U.K. health system, a few of the major changes to the U.S. health system from the PPACA, and then provides a comparison of what the United States may learn from the U.K. health system during the implementation of the U.S.'s new health law, the PPACA.

After a period in the 1990s when the United Kingdom had plummeting quality of its primary care workforce, with overworked, undervalued, and underresourced GPs, similar to the primary care workforce in the United States today, the United Kingdom implemented reforms to the system to encourage the GP system (Doran and Roland, 2010). The U.K.'s clinical quality level was considered subpar, and required an objective performance evaluation, which was the first set of reforms to take place in 1998. Quality-oriented bodies, such as the National Institute of Clinical Excellence (NICE), was instated to provide independent evaluation in the United Kingdom. In comparison, the United States has been 10 years behind in this regard, as this country has focused on similar objectives of clinical quality guidelines and comparative effectiveness research in the PPACA, starting much later, in 2008. Many of the necessary problems with the U.K. system, which produced reform, including a dissatisfied workforce, a government ready for reform, and experience with pay-for-performance (discussed by Doran and Roland (2010)) are also a part of the U.S. health system, suggesting the United States may be able to use the United Kingdom as its example for change. After the late 1990s, the next set of major reforms came up in 2004, with the introduction of the U.K. pay-for-performance system.

The proposed amendments of the U.K's health system in 2004 focused on a number of aspects of the primary care workforce (the GPs) through "reimbursement, physician job satisfaction, recruitment and retention of physicians, and quality of care" (Doran and Roland, 2010). Through a contract lodged between family practices (facilities, rather than physicians) and the government, the new system provided a way to cap hours, if physicians chose to do so, with a penalty paid for not working after hours. A Quality and Outcomes Framework (QOF) provided reimbursement incentives to practices for investment in training, staff, resources, or it could be used by physicians as extra income if they were already meeting all necessary targets. The QOF is at the heart of the major reforms instituted by the United Kingdom.

## *The U.K.'s QOF System*

The United Kingdom has taken a unified approach to targeting the GP population and placing emphasis on performance-based measurement for GPs through the QOF. The QOF is a model of reimbursement based on the ability for practices to meet a total of 146 clinical care indicators, adjusted to the practice's patient mix that meet these indicators. The practices are scored on a point system, to be used to produce comparisons across clinical care in practices in the health system. The QOF payment formula for physicians was lucrative, as the average GP saw increases of 60% in their salaries. A 15%

increase in the number of physicians, positive physician satisfaction results from surveys, and increases in the number of nurses that were employed suggested some of the strengths of the QOF model.

General performance increases were seen in the QOF indicators in the first few years. The worst performing practices also improved at the highest rates. Yet, after the fourth year of the QOF model, in 2008 and 2009, it seemed that a "quality ceiling" was reached, as Doran and Roland (2010) suggest. The new thresholds could not be placed higher, and many practices were already reaching any performance bars that were to be incentivized. Some quality of care improvements were higher than the benchmarks, deriving little-to-no reimbursement for physicians, and producing less motivation to continue achieving results in the QOF. Nonincentivized conditions for the United Kingdom, such as asthma and coronary heart disease, saw declines in the quality of care and performance, though other chronic conditions, such as diabetes did not, suggesting mixed results of nonincentivized conditions in the QOF. Increased referrals to specialists were found to take place, though the difference in the U.S. and U.K. specialist rate (35 versus 13%) may suggest that increases in referrals to specialists may overburden the specialists in the U.S. system more.

Many of the social components of the QOF include changes to the style of practice, through innovative design and technologies that promote active consultations with the patient on a regular basis. Some of the greatest weaknesses of the QOF are that many physicians may be tied to the incentives only in the short run, and that physicians may check off quality of care objectives just to "appear" stronger in their performance than they are (Doran and Roland, 2010). For this reason, accountability is a serious component and requires independent audit of practices to ensure that standards are being met in a fair manner. The social components of the QOF are being followed by the United States through the U.S.'s ACOs (accountable care organizations) and PCMH (patient-centered medical homecare) models, which have similar objectives of person-alized patient-centered outcomes (discussed in greater detail in the next section). The social components of the QOF also show similarities to concierge medicine, which is discussed in the final section before the conclusion. Before suggesting comparisons of the QOF to the U.S. health system, the author analyzes critiques of the QOF from other authors.

## Criticisms of the U.K. Health Reforms and the QOF

Gillam et al. (2012) produced a systematic review detailing the effects of instating a QOF for the United Kingdom. The quality of care indicators within the QOF (that were tied to reimburse-ment incentives) showed direct improvement in the systematic review in the first year. Cost effectiveness was tied to reduc-tions in mortality and hospital admissions in the majority of the nearly 200 articles analyzed. Improved data recording and specialist nursing skills were documented as well. The major disadvantages tied to the QOF were that many of the indica-tors not tied to it actually showed declines, and also declines in patient centeredness and patient satisfaction with continu-ity of care. Overall, the QOF showed modest improvement in chronic conditions, but more time needs to pass to suggest the effects on patient satisfaction, costs, and professionalism.

The QOF also has recently faced negative criticism, as phy-sicians are finding the QOF indicators unrealistic (Pilkington, 2013). A news article by Pilkington in *The Guardian* suggests that extremely high and unrealistic benchmarks in the QOF could be a way that the U.K. government is cutting back on funding GP incentives in the QOF program. Many smaller practices may not have the resources or capital to fund the large-scale changes in the QOF program. This criticism is simi-lar to the state of the PCMH and ACO models in the United States, which are unrealistic for many small practices that cannot put in initial resources, time, and money toward rede-signing their practices for higher quality objectives. The QOF measures also have the disadvantage of penalizing practices with disadvantaged populations and those who serve chronic care populations, because the benchmarks are not likely to improve for practices serving these populations with severe illnesses (Pilkington, 2012).

The United Kingdom has launched reforms that introduce a QOF system that provides pay-for-performance to primary care practices. The QOF has shown important increases to the primary care workforce and increases in salary to the GPs as well. On the other hand, the QOF has felt critiques of its patient satisfaction levels and inability to provide audit control of the QOF. There also seems to be very high QOF measures set, as time has passed, which has made the QOF system less realistic for GPs, and produces less motivation to work on a pay-for-performance system. The next section explores the U.S. health system, and how many of the past and current components compare to the newest reforms in the United Kingdom.

## Comparing and Applying the U.K. to the U.S. Health System

A short overview of the U.S. health system and the new changes to the health system will make comparisons between the U.K. reforms and the U.S. PPACA clearer. The author begins with a short note on the reimbursement scheme of the past U.S. health system, leading up to the latest trends in the PPACA, and then provides comparisons to the U.K. reforms, such as the QOF.

The pre-PPACA U.S. health system has provided three payment options to physicians: fee for service (FFS), which is an individual payment for each service the physician provides to a patient; a capitation fee, which is a fixed amount to the physician's practice; or a salary payment, typically funded by the health system if the physician works for a larger organization

(AARP, 2009). The American Association of Retired Persons produced a report that documented problems with the U.S.'s physician reimbursement plan leading up to the PPACA. It noted that the FFS system has been notorious for its over usage of labor, resources, and more expensive and redundant services. The problems with the FFS system is why the United States has been working toward the PCMH model of care after the passing of the PPACA. Under the traditional U.S. capitation reimbursement system, the current disadvantages have been that physicians are not incentivized to see unhealthy patients, and may delay treatment because they receive only a fixed amount. Finally, salaried reimbursement alone has not been a successful physician remuneration, because it does not promote high levels of productivity (AARP, 2009). Because FFS is the dominant method for reimbursing physicians who participate in Medicare programs, there have been targeted efforts in moving away from FFS to the pay-for-performance system in Medicare programs.

Even after passing the PPACA, no large-scale policies target primary care physicians or their reimbursement system, which is why the U.K. pay-for-performance reforms of 2004 may provide an important guide to the United States, especially the primary care labor force. The U.S. PPACA objectives have primarily targeted specialists and the government insurance programs (Medicare and Medicaid) to be funded and expanded, as well as improved on, through a performance-based measurement system.

Within the United States, California's pay-for-performance system and a few Medicare and non-Medicare programs are the only examples that may closely mirror reforms in the United Kingdom and the U.K. pay-for-performance system (documented by Doran and Roland (2010)). California is one example of a pay-for-performance system, similar to the U.K.'s system. The California system was formed as a way to counter problems with the managed care insurance (HMO and PPO) system. The new California pay-for-performance system produced report cards that provided grades based on objectives and performance-based measures of quality for physician groups in California. The system is difficult to implement in other states, due to disparity in state resources and lack of national initiatives toward such programs.

A few Medicare and non-Medicare programs also have been tied to pay-for-performance, though incentives are not linked to pay-for-performance for the non-Medicare programs. The U.S. pay-for-performance (P4P) model operates similar to the QOF model, though only a portion of the physician's reimbursement payment is based on performance benchmarks, and also may be added to the physician's salary as bonuses (AARP, 2009). Only about 30% of all U.S. physicians were using the P4P model in 2007 (AARP, 2009). There is not enough research to suggest whether P4P has benefits beyond the traditional forms of care. The QOF payment system most resembles the old U.S. system of the capitation fee, and the P4P system because the physician's practice is rewarded based on the standards it meets. The other forms of physician reimbursement that were introduced post-PPACA are the ACOs and PCMH models which are compared to the QOF.

The P4P system in the United States resembles the QOF, but has had difficulties in utilization. Because incentives are not provided to non-Medicare programs, it is difficult to get more of the primary care practices to switch over to the P4P system. The model also only provides the P4P reimbursement amount as a portion of total reimbursement of services, compared to the United Kingdom, where the entire bonus for performance is provided to the practice, regardless of other reimbursement that the practice receives.

The U.S.'s PPACA has produced similar programs to the QOF, such as the ACO and PCMH models. These models are undergoing similar problems as the critiques of the QOF model suggested. Yet, the ACO and PCMH models may be able to learn from the weaknesses of the QOF. The objectives of the U.S. ACOs are tied primarily to Medicare ACO Shared

Savings Program (MSSP). Though the objective is to reduce the shortage of primary care physicians catering to elderly populations, the reach is only for practices that have patients covered under the national Medicare insurance program (Healthcare. gov, 2013; AAFP, 2012). This again makes the scope of coverage limited only to practices with government insured patients, which may not be as effective in targeting all primary care practices. The ACO model can be defined as "multispecialty groups, integrated delivery systems, or loose groups of physicians" who come together because they are incentivized by reimbursement rewards for applying quality care objectives that reduce spending (AARP, 2009). Yet, the ACOs have faced severe problems in incorporating smaller practices because of the lack of capital in smaller practices and the requirement that the practice's patients must be Medicare insured in order to receive incentives. The ACOs may learn from some of the problematic components of the QOF, such as the levels of patient dissatisfaction, and problems with nonincentivized performance-based indicators of quality of care.

The PCMH model in the United States does not focus primarily on objective measures, but its emphasis is practice redesign efforts, which are part of the QOF as well. Some of the social QOF factors of patient-centric outcomes and practice redesign, which are part of the PCMH as well, include "ongoing assistance from a change facilitator, ongoing consultation from a panel of experts in practice economics, health information technology, quality improvement, discounted software technology, training, and support" (Nutting et al., 2009). The PCMH model continues FFS, but reimburses physicians on a monthly basis for practicing with state-of-the-art health information technology (HIT), producing patient-centered outcomes research, and having an innovative redesigned practice (based on specified Institute of Medicine objectives). This parallels the structure of the QOF in the United Kingdom. The QOF also has some similarities to the PCMH model in the United States, because of incentives that are tied to HIT usage and quality of care. Thus, the PCMH model in the United States may be able to learn from the advantages and disadvantages of the U.K.'s QOF framework. One of the major disadvantages to the QOF is the inability to independently audit the organization to verify that clinical objectives are being met, which needs to be a new focus of the PCMH. One way to achieve this may be through automated electronic health records (EHR) reports, once a greater number of small practices in the United States are willing to use EHRs.

QOF reforms were measured through electronic records, because the process quality measurement could be automated through the EHR system. In this regard, the United Kingdom reimbursed anywhere from half to the total cost of the EHR for general practices. The United States can learn from this example, considering that the U.S. "meaningful use" policies target primarily practices with government-insurance patients, rather than all small practices. The United States is not promoting the adoption of electronic health records through incentive systems for small practices; rather, it provides training and support for small practices through state funding of regional extension centers (RECs), which can vary by geographic location and need. The training reimbursement alone is not enough to provide financial and social incentives for small practices to go electronic. Aziz (2012) discusses the major issues that need to change for the current QOF, which also can be applied to the U.S.'s PCMH and ACO models— the need for more time with patients during consultation and greater access to GPs.

The United States and United Kingdom have had different health systems until the introduction of the single payer system in the United States through the PPACA. The QOF, from recent reforms in the United Kingdom, can be paralleled with the capitation and pay-for-performance system in the United States, though they are being implemented differently. The United States has focused primarily on providing pay-for-performance to Medicare eligible practices, though the U.K. system provides the performance reimbursement to all practices that show performance improvement. On the other hand, the newest reforms in the United States from the PPACA, including the presence of ACOs and PCMH models, have similar components to the U.K. pay-for-performance QOF system. The ACOs, though primarily Medicare-oriented, provide similar incentives to the U.K.'s QOF, while the PCMH model has a similar social objective of prevention and patient-centered outcomes to the U.K. QOF. Both the ACOs and the PCMH focus on electronic dissemination of health records, which the QOF also provided funding toward. Yet, the newer models of care may have lessons to learn from the challenges faced by the QOF. The lack of an independent audit on the QOF provides guidance to the United States to have an independent regulatory body when providing performance-based incentives in the ACOs and PCMH. Other problems in the QOF were the faltering non-QOF measures, due to focus on only specific health indicators, and a dissatisfaction of the QOF system by patients. The author also proposes that some of the problems faced by the U.K. QOF may be addressed through the concierge medicine policy solution, which is discussed in the next section.

## Comparisons and Additions of the U.K. QOF to Concierge Medicine

The introduction of concierge medicine to the United States provides a new angle to target some of the problems faced in the U.S.'s primary care shortage. Concierge medicine is seen favorably by many small practices that are struggling to stay in business, and need to reduce administrative struggles, overburdened practices, and over-utilized care. The author first defines concierge medicine, and then discusses how the QOF may be beneficial in producing a stronger concierge medicine system for the United States.

Concierge medicine is a direct relationship between the patient and physician, where the physician promises the patient 24/7, personalized access to care in return for a direct monetary amount (typically on a fee-for-care or fee-for-service basis) (Knope, 2010). Concierge care does not involve a third-party reimbursement policy, so the billing between physician and patient is based primarily on what the patient needs (checkups, physical examinations, lab tests, and so on), rather than insurance billing codes. Because concierge care is relatively new, it is difficult to find guidelines that are specific to quality and quantity of concierge care services. Concierge care is similar to the PCMH in its practice design, as most concierge physicians practice with the latest health technologies, and have patient portals that allow patients to access their own health records. Yet, little is known about the way that concierge physicians measure their own quality of care standards, and many are opposed to the government regulation that is involved in ACOs and PCMH models of care. Concierge practices typically shy away from government-regulated standards and practices (Concierge Medicine Collective, 2012). Taking the strengths and limitations of concierge medicine into consideration, the author points out some of the interesting additions that could be made to the field if the U.K. system and its QOF were included as part of concierge medicine.

The reforms in the U.K. system and the QOF may provide some advantages to the field of concierge medicine if adapted to fit a concierge style of medicine. Some of the most beneficial components of the U.K. system and the QOF system is the use of clinical care guidelines tied to performance. At present, concierge care physicians typically ask for a set fee on an annual or monthly basis, though there is no way to code or bill their time based on a specific category of health services, or set of indicators of care. By instating the QOF, there may be a way to verify the output that is present in concierge care. Similarly, many ethical battles posed against concierge care, including reports by Levy, Conroy, and Schoppmann (2007), suggest that concierge care is currently viewed negatively because of a lack of differentiation between concierge services and traditional insurance billable services. The QOF provides a list of indicators and services that concierge practices could personalize to produce an objective set of guidelines for the care they deliver. Due to the discontent with government regulation, an independent body or framework, similar to the QOF, may provide more clout in the concierge practices, compared to a government body, such as the PCMH, which the concierge practices do not follow. The presence of objective standards of care in concierge practices also may facilitate the research on concierge medicine that is currently lacking. Concierge care already takes into account many of the innovative components of HIT, similar the U.K. QOF, though concierge care utilizes HIT without government incentives. The government Meaningful Use incentives for HIT are only provided to Medicare and Medicaid billable services, which are not part of concierge care. Providing greater incentives to HIT usage also may facilitate and increase the presence of HIT across concierge physicians.

Some of the components that would not be useful to concierge care from the U.K. system include the mandate of core hours for physicians, which is currently part of the U.K. system (Doran and Roland, 2009). In the United Kingdom, GPs have to pay a fee if they don't want to work after hours, or beyond the core hours required. In the concierge system, physicians don't have this "penalty," due to the nature of concierge medicine. The after-hours care is a part of concierge care already, because the presence of a physician providing 24/7 service is a part of the field's added benefits. The need for the U.K.'s Primary Care Trusts system that provides after-hours care also would be unnecessary under concierge care; the system of urgent care clinics similar to the Primary Care Trusts already exists today. Because the field of concierge care is still limited in research, the author provided a few hypothesized additions to the field that may be beneficial from the U.K. system. The majority of the government sponsored (U.K.) reforms will be important to the U.S.'s traditional primary care workforce, until more physicians join concierge medicine. Next, the author provides, as part of the conclusion, a consolidated account of the major ways that traditional primary care in the United States and concierge medicine may benefit from the reforms of the U.K.'s health system.

## Conclusion

The U.K. health reforms of the 1990s and 2000s may be useful as comparisons to the U.S. health system. The economic advantages of a pay-for-performance system with a Quality and Outcome Framework (QOF) may bolster the number of primary care professionals and the incentives for primary care professionals to practice in the United States. The social advantages of the QOF include the incentives provided to all GPs from using health information technology and a patient-centered outcomes model in the practice. The many weaknesses of the QOF model, including problems with auditing the performance-based system for fraud, lack of patient satisfaction, and unrealistic benchmarks over time, may be important lessons for the United States to learn from when applying the QOF to some of the similar programs of the U.S.'s PPACA.

Because of many problems faced in the U.S. health system, the PPACA has presented examples of reforms, such as the ACO model and PCMH, which have advantages and disadvantages. They are similar as well to the QOF model in the United Kingdom in reimbursement of physicians and practice redesign. By analyzing the strengths of the QOF model and problems faced by physicians in this system, the ACO and PCMH model can learn from these examples to improvise their own system. Some of the ways in which the United

States can benefit from the U.K. example of health reforms include the performance-based reimbursement systems of the QOF model, which provides GPs and their clinics with reimbursement for meeting objectives. ACOs are primarily formed around Medicare pay-for-performance, so many small practices may be left out of the ACO models. Building a QOF around the other segment of the small practices that do not have primarily Medicare patients may produce an objective health system. The PCMH model provides a capitation and normal reimbursement to the U.S. GPs as a bonus for meeting quality objectives, in comparison to the U.K. QOF, which ties all GP to pay-for-performance.

Many practice redesign efforts of the PCMH and objectives of patient-centered care outcomes mirror the U.K. health system, so the PCMH model can learn from research on the patient satisfaction levels and professional standards in the QOF. The PCMH is already utilizing the health technologies that the U.K. health system had in its reforms. Concierge care also may benefit from the QOF and U.K. health system by introducing an objective measurement of quality of care and service standards and tying that to reimbursement. Concierge care has been doubted because of its lack of objective policies and reimbursement rates in comparison to other organizations, which is why the QOF may help justify concierge care, while serving as a lucrative means for primary care physicians in the United States. The United States can also learn from the investment in HITs that the United Kingdom has made directly in its small practices, which the United States has only indirectly attempted to do. Overall, by studying the U.K. NHS, the United States can apply the strengths of the U.K.'s health system, while learning from the weaknesses, in building on its current PPACA and primary care policies. This may provide a strong outlook for the state of primary care in this country's future.

# References

AARP. 2009. Physician Payments: Current System and Opportunities for Reform. Retrieved from HYPERLINK "http://assets.aarp.org/rgcenter/health/2009_09_payment.pdf" http://assets.aarp.org/rgcenter/health/2009_09_payment.pdf

Agency for Healthcare Research and Quality (AHRQ). 2012 AHRQ fact sheet: Number of practicing primary care physicians in the U.S. Online at: http://www.ahrq.gov/research/findings/fact-sheets/primary/pcwork1/index.html

American Academy of Family Physicians (AAFP). (2012, February). Data illustrate geographic dispersal of family physicians, other primary care professionals. Online at: http://www.aafp.org/online/en/home/publications/news/news-now/practice-profes-sional-issues/20120203ahrqgeodata.html

Aziz, Z. 2012. GP quality and outcomes framework indicators focus on the wrong issues. *The Guardian,* November 13. Online at: http://www.guardian.co.uk/society/2012/nov/13/gp-quality-outcomes-framework-indicators

Concierge Medicine Collective, & Concierge Medicine News. 2013. *Demand For Concierge Medical Care Currently Outweighs Supply of Physicians Across U.S.* Retrieved from http://www.paragonprivatehealth.com/uploads/Jan._16_2013_-_Concierge_Medicine_News_-Demand_For_Concierge_Medical_Care_Currently_Outweighs_Supply_of_Physicians_Across_U.S..pdf

Doran, T., and M. Roland. 2010. Lessons from major initiatives to improve primary care in the United Kingdom. *Health Affairs* 29 (5): 1023–1029.

Forrest, C. B., Majeed, A., Weiner, J. P., Carroll, K., & Bindman, A. B. 2002. Comparison of specialty referral rates in the United Kingdom and the United States: retrospective cohort analysis. *BMJ,* 325(7360), 370–371. doi:10.1136/bmj.325.7360.370

General Medical Council. 2013. List of registered medical practitioners: Statistics. Online at: http://www.gmc-uk.org/doctors/register/search_stats.asp (accessed May 22, 2013).

Gillam, S. J., A. N. Siriwardena, and N. Steel. 2012. Pay-for-Performance in the United Kingdom: Impact of the Quality and Outcomes Framework—A systematic review. *The Annals of Family Medicine* 10 (5): 461–468.

Healthcare.gov. 2013. The PPACA, May 9. Online at: http://www. healthcare.gov/law/

Knope, S. D. 2010. *Concierge Medicine: A New System to Get the Best Healthcare*. Rowman & Littlefield Pub Incorporated.

Levy, M., K. Conroy, and P. C. Schoppmann. 2007. Understanding issues related to concierge medicine. Online at: http://www.drlaw.com/ Articles/Westchester-Physician— -Understanding-the-Issues-R.aspx

National Health Services (NHS). 2013. About the National Health Service (NHS) in England: NHS Choices, April 18. Online at: http://www.nhs.uk/NHSEngland/thenhs/about/Pages/overview. aspx (accessed May 22, 2013).

Nutting, P. A., W. L. Miller, B. F. Crabtree, C. R. Jaen, E. E. Stewart, and K. C. Stange. 2009. Initial lessons from the first national demonstration project on practice transformation to a patient-centered medical homecare. *The Annals of Family Medicine 7* (3): 254–260.

Organization of Economic Cooperation and Development (OECD). 2008. Health system GP remuneration across nations: Working paper no. 41. Online at: http://www.oecd.org/health/health-systems/41925333.pdf

Organization of Economic Cooperation and Development (OECD). 2012. Briefing Not on the Health System of the U.K. OECD Report. Online at: http://www.oecd.org/unitedkingdom/ BriefingNoteUNITEDKINGDOM2012.pdf

Pilkington, A. 2013. This brutal new system: A GP's take on ATOs and work capability assessments. *The Guardian*, January 4. Online at: http://www.guardian.co.uk/commentisfree/2013/ jan/04/gp-atos-work-capability-assessment

*The Huffington Post*. 2010. Too many doctors, but too few primary care ones. Online at: http://www.huffingtonpost.com/ dr-dennis-gottfried/too-many-doctors-but-too_b_568703.html (accessed May 22, 2013).

# Chapter 11

## Conclusion

### Putting It All Together

This chapter summarizes the major elements of this book and provides a perspective on how the different elements fall together. It highlights some of the key points from each chapter.

**Chapter 1** discussed the major theories that better explain the Patient Protection and Affordable Care Act (PPACA) and Health Information Technology for Economic and Clinical Health (HITECH) Act legislation. The purpose of this chapter was to shed light on similarities and differences between the two pieces of legislation and how they are closely intertwined in healthcare. Currently, the research focuses on the two policies as if they were mutually exclusive. My chapter analyzes the many similarities and differences in theory, objectives, and outcomes from the policies and provides a comprehensive analysis of healthcare reform.

**Chapter 2** outlines the role of electronic government. The chapter explores many of the important influences of various government initiatives in impacting health literacy outcomes, and the new phenomenon of electronic health literacy outcomes. The chapter utilizes a national dataset to describe the perceptions of survey respondents about their interests and concern for quality health information, confidence in health information and health providers, and trust in electronic government initiative. It was found that trust in electronic government has a material impact on the quality and concern for health information.

**Chapter 3** goes into detail about government policies relating to health information technologies, and what has been lacking in some of the financial policies. The chapter identifies some of the public policies and alternatives that may better suit the interests of health providers, especially those that have been underrepresented, and new perspectives of incentivizing those that are underrepresented.

**Chapter 4** draws on individualized solutions to healthcare, including the use of electronic health tools for type 2 (self-inflicted) diabetes.

**Chapter 5** draws on a study of childhood obesity, with a policy analysis of the national-, state-, and local-level initiatives taken so far, and the problems, concerns, and needs for the future. The initiatives also are categorized by their environment, economic, political, and technological impacts.

**Chapter 6** addresses the role of community health centers and health information technology, to suggest how these centers may help those in problematic socioeconomic statuses.

**Chapter 7** details a survey of physicians and their opinions on the use of health information technology (HIT), with implications by geographic region and perception of government in healthcare.

**Chapter 8** goes into greater detail on the meso-, macro-, and micro-level problems in healthcare, relating to health information technology (HIT) use and future technologies, such as mobile health tools and cloud technology.

**Chapter 9** details the presence of geographic disparities across regions in the United States, and some of the technological solutions to this problem.

**Chapter 10** suggests the impacts of primary care workforce in the United States and provides a comparative perspective to reforms in the United Kingdom. It suggests lessons that could be learned from the U.K. reforms and applied to PPACA, and how technology is a part of the solution here, too.

The idea behind this book was to provide an emphasis on various dimensions of society that can work toward improved health outcomes. The focus for the future should be preventative healthcare. So far, we have taken a treatment-based approach in the United States, which has led to a varying set of expensive and ineffective policies. By repositioning our objectives toward prevention, the community can work together in producing cost effectiveness, quality of care, and increased access, potentially achieving all the objectives in the "Iron Triangle" of healthcare. A combination of strong theories, comparative effectiveness research, systematic reviews, and primary and secondary analysis of health data can produce major leaps in the state of our healthcare for the future.

# Index

## N